HOLY LAND REFLECTIONS

A Collection of Inspirational Insights from Israel

YAEL ECKSTEIN

HOLY LAND REFLECTIONS

A Collection of Inspirational Insights from Israel

YAEL ECKSTEIN

INTERNATIONAL FELLOWSHIP OF CHRISTIANS AND JEWS®

Holy Land Reflections:

A Collection of Inspirational Insights from Israel

Copyright 2012© by the International Fellowship of
Christians & Jews, Inc.

All rights reserved.

Unless otherwise noted, all quotations are taken from
the *Holy Bible, New International Version*®, NIV®.
Copyright © 1973, 1978, 1984, 2011 by Biblica, Inc.™
Used by permission. All rights reserved worldwide.

Cover and interior design by Design Corps, Batavia, IL
and Colorado Springs, CO (www.designcorps.us)
Project staff: Art Cooley, Camerin Courtney, Denise
Jones, John LaRue, Betsy Schmitt, Katie Windisch

Published by the *International Fellowship of
Christians & Jews* with offices in Australia, Canada,
Israel, South Korea, and the United States.

ISBN 978-0-9816577-3-8

First printing: 2012

IMAGES CREDITS

Cover:

Temple with Ruins by **Getty Images**

Photo of flags being waved on Jerusalem Day
(also on page viii) by **Ziv Koren**

Photo of bicycles in city (also on page 40) by
Debbi Cooper

Photo of emergency personnel helping
citizens (also on page 84) is from **Isranet**

Back cover: photo by **Debbi Cooper**

Inside back flap: photo by **Debbi Cooper**

Interior:
Page viii: photo by **Ziv Koren**
Page 40: photo by **Debbi Cooper**
Page 84: photo by **Isranet**

All images not indicated otherwise
are from **iStockphoto**

TABLE of CONTENTS

FOREWORD FROM RABBI YECHIEL ECKSTEIN

*E*very parent has hopes and dreams for his or her children, and I am no different. For each of my daughters, I have hoped and prayed that they would develop a deep sense of devotion to God, Israel, and the Jewish people. And I am grateful to *Hashem* [God] that I have seen that fulfilled in each one of them.

It gives me great joy to see my daughter, Yael, embrace with such spirit and passion the mission that has given purpose to my life — building bridges of understanding between Christians and Jews and promoting support for Israel. Yael's ardor and excellence in carrying out this work has been recognized by our Board of Directors, who recently named Yael Senior Vice President and international spokesperson for *The Fellowship*.

Since joining *The Fellowship* in 2005, Yael has been a tireless and gifted ambassador for the organization. She has devoted countless hours to visiting hundreds of *Fellowship*-sponsored programs throughout Israel and around the world. She has touched lives, talking with the elderly and forgotten Holocaust survivor, welcoming the newly arrived Jewish immigrant from Ethiopia, playing with the children who have found a loving home in one of the many *Fellowship*-funded orphanages. She has traveled to the former Soviet Union bringing hope and lifesaving necessities, such as food and medicine, to needy Jews of all ages. Each summer, Yael travels to the United States to visit with *The Fellowship*'s donors, telling them how God's love is expressed to Jews in Israel and worldwide through their generous donations. And, all the while, she tends and cares for her own husband and family — including my grandchildren — imparting to them the rich spiritual heritage of the Jewish people as she raises them in the Holy Land.

It is my hope that in reading *Holy Land Reflections*, you, too, will be touched by the story of Yael's journey these past seven years — her daily life in Israel, the celebrations, the struggles, and the blessings of helping others. As I read through the book, quite frankly, I was in awe. Yael, this book is truly yours — your heartfelt and often very personal thoughts, feelings, and stories.

Thank you, Yael, for a job well done. I am very proud of you and love you so much.

Abba

Rabbi Eckstein

INTRODUCTION

*"How good and pleasant it is
when God's people live together in unity!"*

— PSALM 133:1 —

The writings in *Holy Land Reflections* represent my deepest thoughts and prayers from the past seven years of living in Israel. The struggles, beauty, and growth that I have experienced, from making *aliyah* to raising a family in Jerusalem during times of war and terror, are documented in the pages of *Holy Land Reflections* through stories and images. As you read it, I pray you will feel a bit closer to this beautiful land that I am blessed to call home.

In *Holy Land Reflections* you will discover the beauty of the holidays as my family and I celebrate them in the Holy Land. These special observances are a constant source of inspiration for me. The writings you will find in the *Celebrating* section of the book are my soul's expression of love and thanksgiving to God.

In *Daily Living* you'll catch a glimpse into what it's like to live in a land where the patriarchs and prophets walked, where the stories of the Bible truly come to life. It is a land of faith, where holiness permeates everything, as well as a land of tension, where we know another terrorist attack could be just around the corner. Yet somehow, through it all, we never lose faith in God's promise that He will protect His people.

In *Helping Others*, you'll witness the many ways that needy Jews have been helped through the generosity of Christians and Jews from around the world. Through *The Fellowship*'s programs I have seen biblical prophecies fulfilled as I've welcomed new immigrants from Ethiopia arriving in Israel. I have been overcome with gratitude while distributing food, blankets, and other lifesaving necessities to Holocaust survivors and needy Jews. I have been filled with joy as I've played and talked with orphans who finally have a safe and loving home, thanks to our donors and friends.

Finally, my prayer is that in reading this book you will come away with a renewed sense of your own faith, a deeper connection to Israel and her people, and a stronger commitment to follow God's command to *"love your neighbor as yourself"* (Leviticus 19:18).

With blessings from Jerusalem,

Yael Eckstein

*"Blessed are those who have learned to acclaim you, who walk in the light of your presence,
LORD. They rejoice in your name all day long; they celebrate your righteousness."*

— PSALM 89:15–16 —

CELEBRATING

Celebrating holidays here in the Holy Land is unlike anything else in the world. The holiness of the day is palpable. You can feel it in the very air. Everywhere you turn people are worshiping with sincerity, emotion, and love for God. Because I was born and raised in America before making *aliyah* (immigrating to Israel) with my husband, our family celebrates both American and Israeli holidays. Each celebration brings with it new insights and deep lessons.

While it might be expected that celebrating biblical holidays in Israel is a moving and inspiring experience, you may not realize what profound lessons we learn from celebrating American holidays in Israel. With each celebration, I connect to God in a new way, and the lessons I learn during these annual holidays are endless. I invite you to join in my journey and open your heart to growth and God as you read this first section on *Celebrating* and experience what it means to observe the holidays in the Holy Land. ■

"AND GOD SAID TO HIM [JACOB], 'I AM GOD ALMIGHTY; BE FRUITFUL AND INCREASE IN NUMBER. A NATION AND A COMMUNITY OF NATIONS WILL COME FROM YOU, AND KINGS WILL BE AMONG YOUR DESCENDANTS. THE LAND I GAVE TO ABRAHAM AND ISAAC I ALSO GIVE TO YOU, AND I WILL GIVE THIS LAND TO YOUR DESCENDANTS AFTER YOU.' "

— GENESIS 35:11–12

CELEBRATING THE FRUIT OF OUR LABOR

Here in Israel we don't import many fruits and vegetables, so we eat what is in season. Most of our food is grown on our Holy Land's soil and arrives at our homes within days of being harvested. Often when I pick up a fruit to eat, I recite a blessing over it and reflect on how lucky I am to be eating the fruits of Israel — something my ancestors could only have dreamed about through 2,000 years of exile!

Ancient olive trees tended by Franciscan monks 1900-1910
(Library of Congress)

Once a year, on *Tu B'Shvat*, we recognize the order of the world that God put in motion, something we often take for granted. This one day a year we celebrate the truth that everything in the world is miraculous and God's doing — nothing is mundane. How rare it is that we praise God for turning a seed into a tree or buds into a fruit. But on *Tu B'Shvat* we acknowledge God's handiwork and return all recognition for our wonderful world to Him.

Tu B'Shvat is often referred to as the "new year of the trees." At first this may seem odd. But in Judaism, trees represent spiritual continuity and the yearning of a parent to pass down his traditions and beliefs to his children, a deeply spiritual concept that applies to every generation. When older people toil to plant a tree, they often plant it knowing that they will not live to see the tree bear fruit. Yet they plant it with the intention of their children and grandchildren enjoying and appreciating the result of their labor. So too, when we worship God and perform good deeds, we are planting a seed in the world. Even if we do not see an immediate change in the world from our positive actions, we are confident that the seed of our efforts will one day come to fruition.

Our every act affects the world. That is why God gave us the Bible as a guideline for life — to ensure that the actions we perform help reveal His great kindness, not conceal it. Through eating the fruit from plants and trees planted long ago, *Tu B'Shvat* connects us to the sacrifices, deeds, and intentions of previous generations. That is why it is tradition to eat lots of fruit to celebrate the holiday. We are literally enjoying the fruit of our ancestors' labors and vowing to continue the tradition of preparing the world for future generations.

Raising my family in Jerusalem I realize that my responsibility is more defined than it would have been if I had stayed in the United States. It is my obligation to educate them about our history and rights to this land, and I pray that they will recognize the sacrifice that our ancestors made so that we could call Jerusalem our home.

In 1948 my ancestors planted a tree and named that tree Israel. I am the fruit whom their toils have produced, and my children, God willing, will continue the cycle.

GOING DEEPER FOR CHRISTIANS

Consider your own life. What fruit have you sown? What seeds would you most like to plant among your family, your friends, and your community?

Read also:

• Matthew 7:17–20

• John 15:5

• Galatians 5:22

• Colossians 1:6, 10

• 2 Thessalonians 1:11

FROM THE MOUTHS OF OUR CHILDREN

During the Jewish holiday of *Purim*, the main *mitzvahs* (commandments) of the day are to be in a state of complete happiness, hear the reading of the book of Esther, and give to the needy.

During *Adar* (the month leading up to *Purim*) everywhere you walk in Jerusalem there is loud music playing on the street, dancing and singing, and charity being distributed. I never understood why we are commanded to be happy on *Purim*, because happiness has always come naturally to me during this holiday! Yet this year a sobering experience made me realize how hard it can be to stay happy, and how, even during hard times, we must continue to strive to fulfill God's commandments.

I got up early, excited to begin preparations for the 125 guests we were expecting at our *Purim* meal. Yet when my 11-month-old baby woke up screaming, my excitement faded. Picking him up and feeling his forehead, it was clear that he was very sick and needed a doctor immediately. I took him to the doctor's office, where he was diagnosed with pneumonia and prescribed a strong antibiotic.

Returning home through Jerusalem streets ringing with songs and celebrations in anticipation of *Purim*, it was impossible for me to get in the spirit of the holiday. As I kissed my child and prayed for his recovery, I was overwhelmed with concern for his health.

When I got home, I gave my sweet son his medicine, put him to bed, and began cooking for our *Purim* celebration. Eventually I broke down crying.

Dancing during Purim (IFCJ)

It was all too much for me. How could I possibly celebrate when I was so worried about my son?

Then my three-year-old daughter came innocently dancing into the kitchen. She took one look at my red puffy eyes and hugged me. "Mommy," she lovingly whispered, "you shouldn't cry. God commanded us to be happy today!" Her words stopped me. She was right. The commandment to be happy on *Purim* was applicable during good times *and* bad. If we were supposed to be happy only when things were going right, the commandment wouldn't be needed.

Wiping away the tears, I told my daughter to turn on the music very loud. Together we cooked for our guests while dancing, singing, laughing, and praying. As I forced myself to be happy, I realized that fulfilling God's will really does make you feel better!

As I look back, my heart fills with gratitude. I am grateful that my son is feeling better, and that my precious daughter, through her simple words, taught me this ultimate truth: No matter how challenging it is sometimes to fulfill God's commandments, it is always worth doing, since He sent them to us to enhance our lives and to better the world.

GOING DEEPER FOR CHRISTIANS

How does obeying God's word fill you with joy? How can you rejoice in all circumstances, during good times and bad?

Read also:

• Philippians 3:1; 4:4

• 1 Thessalonians 5:16

THE HOPE OF PASSOVER

During Passover in Israel, Jews once again gather to relive the exodus, the story of their ancestors' deliverance from slavery to freedom in biblical times. Though it is an ancient story and Jews have celebrated Passover for thousands of years, even today this sacred holiday gives me much-needed hope when I look at the dire state of our world, so filled with hate, conflict, and anti-Israel sentiment.

When the Israelites were in exile in Egypt, it appears as if God hid His face from them. Although we have no record of miracles performed while they were enslaved, we read the rest of the Passover story and realize that God's love was always present. At the proper time, He took the Jews out of Egypt and brought them to freedom, performing

> "THE LORD HIMSELF GOES BEFORE YOU AND WILL BE WITH YOU; HE WILL NEVER LEAVE YOU NOR FORSAKE YOU. DO NOT BE AFRAID; DO NOT BE DISCOURAGED."
>
> — DEUTERONOMY 31:8

Pyramids in Egypt (IFCJ)

miracles and wonders for the Egyptians to see.

The slavery and hardships experienced by the Jewish people before God freed them from bondage can serve to remind us that even during the rough points in life, God has not forsaken us. When we hit rock bottom and feel utter despair — as the Israelites felt during their torturous slavery — we must remember that our current suffering could be a precursor to freedom, joy, and fulfillment.

Whenever I feel fearful about living in Israel and being surrounded by enemies, I read the story of Passover and my faith is restored. I am reminded that although times look bleak at the moment, God can change the situation in an instant and bring us to beautiful redemption. Learning from the story of Passover, I know that God is always with me and showering me with love — even when times are difficult.

Commemorating the exodus from Egypt is an effective way to strengthen our faith, and it provides us with the spiritual and practical tools we need to overcome hardships and retain faith in an all-loving God. My prayer this Passover is that the love and glory of God will shine strong throughout the world as it did when He took the Jews out of Egypt and brought them to the Holy Land.

May we remember this Passover — and always — that God loves us, is present with us, and is calling us to open our hearts and let Him dwell inside.

GOING DEEPER FOR CHRISTIANS

In what ways has God seen you through a difficult time? Share your story with someone you know who is struggling right now.

Read also:

• Matthew 28:20

• Hebrews 13:5

" 'SURELY THE DAY
IS COMING; IT WILL
BURN LIKE A FURNACE.
ALL THE ARROGANT
AND EVERY EVILDOER
WILL BE STUBBLE,
AND THE DAY THAT
IS COMING WILL SET
THEM ON FIRE,' SAYS
THE LORD ALMIGHTY.
'NOT A ROOT OR A
BRANCH WILL BE LEFT
TO THEM. BUT FOR
YOU WHO REVERE MY
NAME, THE SUN OF
RIGHTEOUSNESS WILL
RISE WITH HEALING
IN ITS RAYS. AND
YOU WILL GO OUT
AND FROLIC LIKE
WELL-FED CALVES.' "

— MALACHI 4:1–2

A SOLEMN CEREMONY AT *YAD VASHEM*

The time leading up to Holocaust Remembrance Day is always very emotional for me. I use it to study some of the individual stories of Jews who perished under horrific conditions during the Holocaust. I interview Holocaust survivors and marvel at the astounding strength it must have taken to rebuild their lives after suffering such incredible hardship. It pains me to think about how many individual life stories, and entire family trees, were lost in the gas chambers.

The stories I hear put faces on the six million — the unfathomable number of Jews killed during this terrible time in history. And every year I am haunted by the reality that the few Holocaust survivors living today are growing old. Although I have been privileged to hear their heroic stories firsthand, my children, unfortunately, will not.

I remember my teacher in middle school trying to teach the students how large the number six million is. Beginning at noon on Holocaust Remembrance Day, a digital clock was set at the entrance of our classrooms that began to count up to six million seconds. Each second that the clock ticked represented another Jewish life that was taken by the Nazis. It took the clock over two full months to reach six million.

I remember staring at the clock, wondering which second represented my family members who were murdered in the Holocaust. I would always thank God that one of those family members — my grandfather — miraculously escaped Nazi Germany by hiding in the forest for months on end with his three siblings and his pregnant mother.

Even as an adult, the systematic murder of six million people in just over a decade is difficult to grasp. To reach six million casualties, the horrors of 9/11 would need to be repeated daily for years, God forbid. In 2009, the entire population of the state of Colorado did not come close to six million. There are not even six million Jews currently living in the United States. Even harder to comprehend is how so much of the world could have stood by while six million Jews were being slaughtered. And I wonder if the same thing could happen today.

For more than 60 years the Jewish people have been blessed with a Jewish homeland in the biblical Promised Land. We have a flourishing army, a democratic government, and — most importantly — an awesome God on our side. I pray that on Holocaust Remembrance Day the world will take the lessons of the Holocaust to heart and collectively call out with one voice to Iran's leaders and all others who threaten Israel's existence: "Never again!"

An Auschwitz survivor (James Nubile)

GOING DEEPER FOR CHRISTIANS

As a Christian, what do you think your response should be to the events of the Holocaust? Consider how you can become part of the healing process.

Read also:

• Matthew 5:9

• Revelation 21:24–26; 22:1–3

PROTECTING THOSE WHO PROTECT US

"BLESSED ARE THOSE WHO HAVE REGARD FOR THE WEAK; THE LORD DELIVERS THEM IN TIMES OF TROUBLE. THE LORD PROTECTS AND PRESERVES THEM — THEY ARE COUNTED AMONG THE BLESSED IN THE LAND — HE DOES NOT GIVE THEM OVER TO THE DESIRE OF THEIR FOES."

— PSALM 41:1–2

Here in the Holy Land, we celebrated Israel Memorial Day. The entire country stood unified as we paid our deepest respects to the young soldiers who gave their lives to protect the Jewish people in our homeland. All day on the radio, we heard the inspiring life stories of the deceased, mothers crying, and spouses eulogizing. As a nation we mourned together for the lives that could have been.

IDF soldiers at Western Wall (ISRANET)

Throughout Memorial Day, I prayed for a group of soldiers I met recently on an army base that *The Fellowship* "adopted." Through this amazing new program, we provide funds to help immigrant soldiers who came to Israel alone. These young men and women have no families to give them support and comfort. Funds also go to help soldiers' needy families.

I couldn't stop thinking about the soldiers at the base. I remembered the young man with side curls and a *kippah* (skull cap) who stood on guard at the entrance carrying his big machine gun in case terrorists tried to infiltrate the base.

The eyes of one young Ethiopian woman soldier who was practicing what to do in case of a chemical attack are still vivid in my mind. Visiting this army base, I felt inspired that Jews from all four corners of the world were preparing to face terror, war, and natural disaster, obediently standing united as guardians of Israel.

The soldiers at the base are on the frontlines of terror. The base is situated just two miles away from Gaza, where Hamas terrorists fire rockets on a near daily basis and dig underground tunnels in hopes of infiltrating Israel. Because of the serious threat, when I arrived at the base the first information I received was the location of the nearest bomb shelter. Pointing to a concrete building a long block away, the commander told me that if a "code red" signal sounded, I would have 12 seconds to get to safety before a rocket strike. "There is no way I will make it there in time!" I replied with fear. "Then get down on the ground and pray," was his blunt response.

Thank God, during my visit there were no rocket or mortar attacks. Yet in the week prior, two rockets landed on site, and there have been numerous attacks since. The one thread of hope and encouragement that the Israeli soldiers hold on to amidst the terror is the knowledge that they are not alone. They find comfort in the fact that Christians and Jews in America, through *The Fellowship*, strongly stand with the Israeli soldiers and will never let them down.

My visit to the army base was a sobering experience. Yet it was also reassuring to see that Israelis are prepared to face whatever threat they may encounter. They are able to do this with no small thanks to the prayers and support of our faithful *Fellowship* friends. God bless you for making this possible.

GOING DEEPER FOR CHRISTIANS

Write a letter or send an e-mail to someone you know who has served in the military, letting him or her know how grateful you are for his or her sacrifice and service.

Read also:

• John 10:14–15; 15:13

• Philippians 2:17

• 1 John 3:16

"The Nation of Israel Lives"

> "I AM WITH
> YOU AND WILL
> WATCH OVER YOU
> WHEREVER YOU GO,
> AND I WILL BRING
> YOU BACK TO THIS
> LAND. I WILL NOT
> LEAVE YOU UNTIL
> I HAVE DONE
> WHAT I HAVE
> PROMISED YOU."
>
> — GENESIS 28:15

Each year, when spring emerges, Israel's Independence Day, *Yom Ha'atzmaut*, comes around and reaffirms our bond to the land, people, and the God of Israel. As this day approaches I take a few moments to reflect on this wonderful and holy land that I have been blessed to call home.

As the biblical homeland of the Jewish people, Israel possesses many qualities that make it unique. For me, life in Israel is as close to paradise as I can imagine. The Israeli flags that line every public street and wave proudly from private homes in the weeks leading up to *Yom Ha'atzmaut* assure me that the pride and love I have for my country is shared by all.

The people in Israel are family, which gives everyone a feeling of safety. Children play outside by themselves, take public buses alone from a young age, and have independence that I have yet to see anywhere else in the world. They feel comfortable and safe asking strangers for help. In fact, in Israel, we don't teach our children not to talk to strangers, but simply to ask strangers for help if they need it.

Another unique aspect of life in Israel is the sanctity of God's word. For instance, there is no place in the world where *Shabbat* (the Sabbath) is as closely observed. In my community on *Shabbat*, families take time to eat together, pray, and study the Bible. The streets are quiet with a holy silence — often the only sounds heard are prayers coming from the nearest synagogue and children laughing as they play special *Shabbat* games. Most businesses shut down, enabling each person to enjoy the day of rest without worrying about daily responsibilities. By sanctifying *Shabbat*, strong family values are instilled from a young age.

(Debbi Cooper)

When I walk the streets of Israel before *Yom Ha'atzmaut*, I realize we have much to be proud of. For more than 60 years, we have survived as a Jewish nation in our biblical homeland, and we have kept our national spirit alive as well. Terrorists have tried to destroy us from the moment the State of Israel was formed in 1948 by attacking us, but the people of Israel remain undaunted.

There are words we live by, words that sound in our souls constantly and are sung by our children in prayer: *Am Yisrael Chai* ("The nation of Israel lives"). That unwavering conviction will keep us celebrating *Yom Ha'atzmaut*, our Day of Independence, and flying our flags proudly in our beautiful, holy country for many years to come.

GOING DEEPER FOR CHRISTIANS

Think about your own country, community, or neighborhood. What makes you proud of where you live? How can you imbue it with a sense of holiness?

Read also:

• Acts 17:26–27

• Ephesians 2:19–20

• Philippians 3:20

EVERY DAY IS MOTHER'S DAY

My amazing and wonderful husband made a mistake many a father has made in the past: He forgot Mother's Day. There were no flowers, no smells of breakfast cooking in the kitchen, no beautifully wrapped presents awaiting me when I woke up. I must admit that I was initially a little disappointed. Yet after praying about it, I realized that Mother's Day is celebrated every day in our home, thanks to the biblical values we live by.

A biblically-centered home builds its foundation on family values, and that is exactly what my husband and I yearn to foster. All the traditions we observe are meant to communicate a message to our children about the sanctity of marriage, the holiness of life, and the greatness of God.

Each week on *Shabbat* (the Sabbath), my husband practices the ancient tradition of singing to me the beautiful, poetic verses of Proverbs 31 that describe the characteristics of "*a wife of noble character.*" Having heard this biblical song their whole life, my children already know it by heart. They watch intently as my husband sings, and then we begin our *Shabbat* meal.

In this age it is not easy to educate and inspire our children to follow in biblical ways. But Proverbs 31 shows children the universal traits that a holy woman possesses — and, of course, so many of the qualities in these timeless verses apply to men also! So, when my husband comes to the verse that reads, "*She opens her arms to the poor and extends her hands to the needy*" (v. 20), we turn to our children and sing this verse to them. This is an ancient truth that we pray they will always remember: that those who wish to live a righteous, godly life should focus their lives on helping people in need.

So as Mother's Day came to an end, I felt no disappointment. I found I didn't miss having flowers on the table. Instead, I thanked God for the deep love and appreciation of my family. And I thank Him as well for the biblical values that He gave to us, His children, as guidelines for living and for a family that, by adhering to those values, makes every day feel like the best Mother's Day in the world.

Woman and child at Western Wall (Debbi Cooper)

GOING DEEPER FOR CHRISTIANS

Read Proverbs 31 with your family or friends. Talk about the values and characteristics of "a wife of noble character." Share which of the characteristics you see in each other.

Read also:

• Acts 9:36–42

• 1 Timothy 2:9–10

• 1 Peter 3:3–6

THE MIRACLE OF JERUSALEM

"THE LORD GIVES
VICTORY TO HIS
ANOINTED.
HE ANSWERS HIM
FROM HIS HEAVENLY
SANCTUARY WITH
THE VICTORIOUS
POWER OF HIS
RIGHT HAND.
SOME TRUST IN
CHARIOTS AND
SOME IN HORSES,
BUT WE TRUST IN
THE NAME OF THE
LORD OUR GOD."

— PSALM 20:6–7

Jerusalem Street in Old City 1920-1933
(Library of Congress)

Mount Herzl is a military cemetery and war memorial in Jerusalem that symbolizes both sacrifice and hope to the people of Israel. On Jerusalem Day, I went to pay my respects and learn a little more about this amazing country that I am blessed to call home.

As I ascended the mountain that overlooks ancient and modern Jerusalem, I glimpsed families carrying pictures of teenage children. At first, I couldn't understand why. But when I entered the cemetery it became clear. The ages on the graves showed that many of the soldiers buried here were very young when they had died. The pictures that everyone was holding on Mount Herzl were of loved ones lost in the wars for Israel's survival — the true heroes and ultimate servants of God.

The holy homeland of the Jewish people is surrounded by millions of terrorists and enemies sworn to our destruction. For this reason, army service

16

is mandatory for every young Israeli. Looking at the list of seemingly endless wars that Israel has fought in such a short period of time, I thought of my relatives and friends who are currently serving in the Israeli army and the dangers they face, and I had to sit down to catch my breath.

Of course, Israel relies on more than military might to defend herself. The only way to live in a country that is an island of light in a sea of darkness is to be steadfast in your faith. The Israeli people, who live in God's chosen land and fight in His righteous army, make all decisions based on faith and rely on miracles for our survival.

The 1967 Six-Day War, which reunified the Jewish people with our blessed capital, was one such miracle. Each time I see pictures taken during the war of Israeli soldiers praying at the Western Wall for the first time since 1948, overwhelming joy and thanksgiving well up inside my heart.

As the sun set and Jerusalem Day came to an end, thousands of Jewish youth continued to walk the streets waving the Israeli flag with pride. Although it was late at night, the air was filled with the sound of biblically-based songs celebrating a Jewish Jerusalem. On the radio, I heard Israeli pop songs whose lyrics are based on ancient prayers relating to the Jews returning home.

Jerusalem Day is observed only one day a year, but the sentiments expressed on that day live in the heart of every Jewish person at every moment. We yearn for a peaceful Jerusalem, but if forced to, we will fight. We have finally returned home, after 2,000 years, and we are not leaving again.

GOING DEEPER FOR CHRISTIANS

What is most important to your sense of security? Is it a well-managed financial portfolio? A home alarm system? What role does your faith play in making you feel secure?

Read also:

• 1 Corinthians 1:8; 15:2

• Hebrews 6:19

• 2 Peter 3:17–18

"I WILL ESTABLISH
MY COVENANT AS
AN EVERLASTING
COVENANT BETWEEN
ME AND YOU AND
YOUR DESCENDANTS
AFTER YOU FOR THE
GENERATIONS TO COME,
TO BE YOUR GOD AND
THE GOD OF YOUR
DESCENDANTS AFTER
YOU. THE WHOLE LAND
OF CANAAN, WHERE
YOU NOW RESIDE AS A
FOREIGNER, I WILL GIVE
AS AN EVERLASTING
POSSESSION TO
YOU AND YOUR
DESCENDANTS AFTER
YOU; AND I WILL BE
THEIR GOD."

— GENESIS 17:7–8

CELEBRATING JERUSALEM DAY!

My family heritage dates back eight generations in Jerusalem — hundreds of years before the modern State of Israel was even established! Jerusalem truly runs through my blood, and it is the only place in the world that feels like home. As a Jewish woman, I know that God has clearly proclaimed through the Bible that Israel is my true home.

It is hard to believe that up until 1967 Jerusalem was not fully under Jewish rule — Jordan still controlled East Jerusalem. After God performed six days of miracles for His children, the city of Jerusalem was reunited for the Jewish people and the world to witness.

Many stories from the 1967 war have been passed down through the generations, but there is one that inspires me and reminds me that the prophets I read about in the Bible are ever present in the land of our forefathers.

The Israeli soldiers who fought to free Jerusalem told of a miraculous occurrence when they first entered the Old City during the fighting in 1967. As the soldiers came through a back entrance, they stopped to pray at the grave of Samuel the prophet. Even as bullets flew overhead, the soldiers said a quick prayer for success before they then proceeded to liberate Jerusalem from enemy hands. As it turns out, the same day Israel succeeded in reuniting Jerusalem was also the anniversary of Samuel's death.

This story of faith and prayer reminds me that in Jerusalem there is no such thing as chance — in good times and in bad, in times of war and

Israeli paratroopers after capturing Western Wall in 1967
(Photo courtesy of the Israeli Government Press Office)

peace, everything resonates with holiness and biblical significance. Each year that I celebrate Jerusalem Day, I thank God that I am free to worship at the Wailing Wall, visit the graves of our prophets, walk the Mount of Olives, and witness biblical prophecy being fulfilled.

This year is a special Jerusalem Day celebration for me because I am spending it with my *Saba* and *Savta* (grandmother and grandfather), who are 84 and 91 years old, respectively. They recently made *aliyah* (immigrated to Israel) from the United States and now call Jerusalem home. Although my grandfather was born in Jerusalem, his family left Israel when he was young. His prophetic homecoming means that there are now four generations of the Eckstein family living in our biblical homeland.

I am so proud and grateful to God that my family has the amazing opportunity to take part in the biblical prophecy of the ingathering of God's children.

GOING DEEPER FOR CHRISTIANS

Where do you feel most connected to your heritage and family roots? Where do you feel most connected to the family of God?

Read also:

• John 1:12

• Romans 8:15–16

• Galatians 4:5–6

• Ephesians 3:14–16

CELEBRATING *Shavuot*

"THE DECREES OF
THE LORD ARE FIRM,
AND ALL OF THEM
ARE RIGHTEOUS.
THEY ARE MORE
PRECIOUS THAN
GOLD, THAN MUCH
PURE GOLD; THEY
ARE SWEETER THAN
HONEY, THAN
HONEY FROM THE
HONEYCOMB.
BY THEM YOUR
SERVANT IS WARNED;
IN KEEPING THEM
THERE IS GREAT
REWARD."

— PSALM 19:9b–11

*S*havuot in Jerusalem is truly magical. On this important holiday, Jews commemorate the time in ancient days when the "first fruits" were harvested and brought to the Temple in Jerusalem as an offering to God. It is also a celebration of the glorious day when God gave us the *Torah* (the first five books of the Hebrew Bible) on Mount Sinai. While *Shavuot* is special to Jews all over the world, I must say that having the blessing of celebrating the holiday in Jerusalem is beyond compare!

Jewish holidays allow us to take a break from our daily cares and worries and to set aside time for introspection. I did all of the physical preparation of cooking and cleaning for *Shavuot* the day before the holiday began, so that I could enter the holiday free from worldly worries.

As the sun set, the streets of Jerusalem were packed with

Teenage boy studying the Torah *with older man* (Debbi Cooper)

people dressed in their most beautiful clothes making their way to synagogue. From each block the sound of singing and dancing filled the air. Children stayed up late to join the festivities and were eating candies and sweets to represent the sweetness of the *Torah*. At our house we welcomed family members from all over the country for dinner. The mood was one of gratitude to God for giving us the most precious gift possible: the Bible.

Jewish tradition holds that the *Torah* was received in the morning. Therefore, on *Shavuot*, it has become the custom to stay up all night learning and praying in anticipation of the big event. At my synagogue, Bible classes took place from 11:30 p.m. until sunrise. I attended one class and then walked with my husband, daughter, and thousands of others to the Western Wall in the Old City of Jerusalem, which Jews believe is the spiritual center of the world.

Many people flocked from all over Israel to study *Torah* at the Wall throughout the night. In fact, there were so many people that it felt like the middle of the day, even though it was 3 a.m.! Everyone wanted to get a little closer to God's presence, just like in biblical times when Jewish people were commanded to ascend to the Temple three times a year and bring a holy sacrifice. One of those times was *Shavuot*.

The feeling of unity I experienced standing at the Western Wall made me think of many moments in the history of my people: how God parted the Red Sea, allowing them to escape Pharaoh's army after they were freed from Egypt; how they walked in the desert to Mount Sinai to receive the *Torah*; how they entered into Israel, the land promised them by God.

I reflected on how Israel today faces many challenges, just as it did in biblical times, and how the secret to our facing those challenges is always the same: to trust in God, to ask Him for guidance, and to listen for His voice through His word.

GOING DEEPER FOR CHRISTIANS

Reflect on the gift of God's word in your own life. In what ways has God's word guided and helped you through challenges?

Read also:

• Luke 11:28

• 2 Timothy 3:16–17

• Hebrews 4:12

HAPPY FATHER'S DAY

Rabbi Yechiel Eckstein and Yael Eckstein in Jerusalem
(IFCJ)

Happy Father's Day! As I sit here in Jerusalem, now a mother myself, I can't help reliving and reflecting on some of the amazing memories I have after 25 years as your daughter. From "Sunday-Funday" at Six Flags Amusement Park to curling up on your lap as a little girl while you sang songs on the Sabbath, your fatherly presence has always been an integral part of my life.

Despite all the demands on your time, family has always been your top priority. When I was a child, you never missed a school play, and you were never too busy to attend a birthday party. You raised your three daughters with the values of charity, spirituality, and sensitivity — holy attributes that I am now passing on to my children. And, today, though you do lots of traveling around the world, I never feel like you are very far away. Hardly a day goes by without an optimistic and encouraging phone call from you. Your voice alone brightens my day.

22

Although our relationship has changed throughout the years — I've gone from being your little baby to having babies myself — our connection has only grown. Because of the support you give me, I feel there is no challenge too big for me to face. I know you are behind me every step of the way, and I have no fears of falling, because I know you are always there to catch me. I have the confidence to follow my dreams and my heart because you believe in me.

You were always my role model. Then, I moved to Israel and saw firsthand the thousands of people being helped by *The Fellowship*; seeing that increased my admiration of you and my appreciation for your lifelong dream. I see now that your dream is being realized: strengthening the State of Israel, helping Jews in need around the world, and bridging the gap between Christians and Jews.

Your accomplishments, Abba, are many — too many to list here — and yet your children are your greatest pride and joy. Today, I want you to know how much I recognize and appreciate all of your exceptional traits. You are an amazing father, grandfather, and man. You treat every needy and hurting person you come across with respect and care. From you, I have learned the meaning of true kindness and charity. I know that I am a better person because of your influence. I have learned, and continue to learn, more from you than you can ever imagine. My love for you only grows.

So, on this Father's Day, feel proud of the father that you have been and know that your children love you without end. You are our best friend and our role model, and will always continue to be.

GOING DEEPER FOR CHRISTIANS

What lessons have you learned from your father or father figure? What spiritual legacy would you like to leave for others?

Read also:

- Acts 2:38–40

- Ephesians 6:1, 4

- Colossians 3:20

A Shared Celebration of Freedom

"THE SPIRIT OF THE
SOVEREIGN LORD
IS ON ME, BECAUSE
THE LORD HAS
ANOINTED ME TO
PROCLAIM GOOD
NEWS TO THE POOR.
HE HAS SENT ME
TO BIND UP THE
BROKENHEARTED,
TO PROCLAIM
FREEDOM FOR THE
CAPTIVES AND
RELEASE FROM
DARKNESS FOR
THE PRISONERS."

— ISAIAH 61:1

Although I left America, the country of my birth, more than seven years ago to make *aliyah* (immigrated to Israel), I am still a strong American patriot. I'm proud to hold dual American and Israeli citizenship, and greatly appreciate the "land of the free and the home of the brave" for all of the virtues it brings to this confused and often morally bankrupt world. Each July 4, I pray that the United States will be blessed with peace and prosperity, and my heart sings out psalms of thanksgiving to God for the unbreakable American–Israeli alliance.

Growing up in the United States, I was able to feel proud of my Jewish identity. This taught me that freedom breeds a healthy respect for diversity. Unlike so many countries around the world — and especially in the Middle East — in America, freedom of religion is a foundational value. Respect for all individuals, whatever their race or religion, is a significant achievement for mankind, and it was in the United States that this principle was developed to its fullest expression.

The Judeo-Christian values that are the source of so much good in the world are upheld in America, and I am confident that this brings joy to our holy God. I have faith in my heart that each time an American child says the Pledge of Allegiance, which refers to the United States as "one nation under God," it opens up heavenly channels for blessings. Everything that the Bible tells us pleases God — virtues like charity, kindness, and faith — is upheld as an ideal in American society.

In Israel, the night skies light up with fireworks on the Fourth of July. As America's strongest ally, Israel celebrates American independence with joy and thanksgiving. The Israeli people stand together with the American people in the war against terror, and we are proud to be on the frontlines fighting to keep the free world safe. Here in the Holy Land, when we fight terrorism, we know that we are doing our part to keep America safe as well — just as when America eliminates an arch-terrorist like Osama bin Laden, it is striking a blow in defense of Israel's security.

America represents freedom, and that is what we celebrate — Israelis and Americans — on the Fourth of July. God bless America, land that I love.

GOING DEEPER FOR CHRISTIANS

Share with family or friends three reasons why you love your country. What freedoms do you value the most?

Read also:

• John 8:35–36

• Romans 8:21

• 2 Corinthians 3:17

• Galatians 4:3–5

REFLECTIONS ON *TISHA B'AV* — A TIME FOR MOURNING

"They burned
your sanctuary
to the ground;
they defiled the
dwelling place of
your Name.
They said in
their hearts, 'We
will crush them
completely!'
They burned
every place
where God was
worshiped in the
land."

— PSALM 74:7–8

The Jewish fast day of *Tisha B'Av* (meaning the ninth day of the Hebrew month of *Av*), which Jews worldwide observe, commemorates the destruction of the First and Second Temples in Jerusalem on this very day — the first time in 586 B.C.E., the second in 70 C.E. It is a solemn day that we mark each year with mourning, fasting, and praying. Leading up to *Tisha B'Av* are three weeks of introspection and semi-mourning, corresponding to the three weeks between the time that the Temple walls were breached until it was destroyed completely.

During this period I often go to the Western Wall — the last remaining portion of the Second Temple — to reflect on what the Temple's destruction means to me. As I stood by the Wall, immersed in prayer, I thought about how we are commanded to mourn for the Temple until it is rebuilt.

Yael Eckstein at the Western Wall (Debbi Cooper)

There is a wonderful Jewish teaching that whoever truly mourns the Temple's destruction will merit seeing it rebuilt. This compels me to want to feel the pain of living in an unredeemed world without the Temple, yet sometimes even that reality is difficult to really experience.

Opening my eyes and staring at the holy Wall, I realized that I was standing next to an old Jewish woman who was weeping while praying. She laid her head on the Wall and cried out between her tears, "Why, God, why?" I stood staring at her, and very quickly tears started falling down my face as well. I saw so much pain, along with so much faith, in this woman. I started calling out the same thing: "Why, God? Why is there so much pain and suffering in this world?" That is when I got on my knees and truly mourned the destruction of the Holy Temple and prayed for its restoration.

In fact, Jews worldwide pray daily for the Temple to be rebuilt, and I have faith that God hears those prayers. Yet I also know that God is looking for action in us, His children. We are taught that the Temple was destroyed because of the sin of baseless hatred, and I believe that it will be rebuilt only when we reverse that sin and begin loving each other completely. The Temple is God's way of showing us, His children, that He loves us and wants to have a presence and dwelling place in our midst. But how can He — the God of peace — dwell in this world if there is hate in our hearts?

And so, during the three weeks leading up to *Tisha B'Av*, I have decided to do my part in rebuilding the Temple and bringing God's presence in the world as best I can. I am trying to be more sensitive toward other people's needs, to be kind, and to help others every opportunity I get. I pray that one day *Tisha B'Av* will be marked not with mourning but with celebration and love among all God's children.

GOING DEEPER FOR CHRISTIANS

In what ways can mourning over our sin and hurtful actions lead to changed behavior? What is causing you to grieve now? How can you use that grief to make a positive change?

Read also:

• John 16:20

• 2 Corinthians 7:9–10

• James 4:8–10

Preparing for the New Year

"Comfort, comfort my people, says your God."

— Isaiah 40:1

*R*osh Hashanah, the Jewish New Year, inspires in me a deep longing to grow closer to God. In preparation for the holiday, on which tradition holds that we are judged individually for the good and bad deeds of the previous year, I focus my energies on prayer, repentance, and charity. Growing closer to God always gives me a sense of security and warmth, and enables me to welcome the New Year with confidence and joy. Obeying God's word makes me feel blessed to be alive, as I partner with Him in fulfilling His biblical will.

Children in Israel learn very early about *Rosh Hashanah* in school and help make beautiful New Year's cards for Holocaust survivors and sick children. The biblical concept of standing together in love and prayer is instilled in Israeli children from a young age, as they help deliver food boxes to the needy and donate clothes to the poor.

All over the country, children bake cookies for the Israeli soldiers who must defend the Holy Land's borders over the holiday, and deliver the goodies to them with appreciation for their service. Whenever I fear for Israel's future, I look around at the values instilled in the children of Israel, and I know we will persevere.

Amazingly, it is not only the Israeli people who have stood unified to provide for the weakest of Israeli society, but also the Christian community in America and Canada as well. Leading up to the holiday, I have been busy delivering *Fellowship*-funded food boxes to thousands of needy families who would otherwise be hungry, and providing new clothing and shoes to orphans.

Yael Eckstein helps with food distribution (Yossi Zamir)

Seeing their faces light up after reading the *Fellowship* New Year's card, which explains that this is a holiday gift from Christians in America, is priceless. I'll never forget watching eight-year-old Tamar open the food box for her family. After seeing that they wouldn't go hungry that *Rosh Hashanah*, she broke down crying. "It is because of *The Fellowship* that I can enter this *Rosh Hashanah* with a feeling of hope," she said.

The biblical and prophetic work of *The Fellowship* is spreading courage, comfort, and yes, hope, throughout the Holy Land, and letting Israel's people know that they are not alone.

The prevalent and lifesaving acts of charity and kindness that are being done in Israel through the *International Fellowship of Christians and Jews* enable the people of Israel to welcome the New Year in high spirits and thanksgiving to God. We are thankful for the hope given to the desolate, food for the hungry, and compassion for the orphaned that is expressed during this holiday season and throughout the year.

Wishing you a *shana tova u'mitukah* — a happy and sweet New Year!

GOING DEEPER FOR CHRISTIANS

What gives you hope during difficult times? In what ways can you spread hope to others?

Read also:

• 2 Corinthians 1:3–5

• Philippians 2:1–2

• Colossians 3:12

• 1 Peter 3:8

Shana Tova — Happy New Year!

Another year has passed, and *Rosh Hashanah* has arrived once again. I feel blessed to have two days to set aside as a time of reflection. Too often my life is so hectic that I rarely have time to simply focus on the goodness that God has bestowed on me and the world. The two days of *Rosh Hashanah* are a time to examine the past year and set goals for the future. On these days, we pray that God will give us the strength and vision that we need to improve ourselves and our surroundings in a holy manner.

The world turns with the cycles that God created. Just as God created the four seasons, each with its own characteristics, He also created in the spiritual world holy days with their own unique energy. He created Passover with a focus on personal redemption and *Rosh Hashanah* with the blessing of new beginnings. Each holiday is a unique gift from God.

Jewish tradition holds that on *Rosh Hashanah* God signs each person's name in the Book of Life or Death for the coming year; on *Yom Kippur* that fate is sealed. As a little girl, I remember running around doing good deeds before *Rosh Hashanah*. I would ask forgiveness from my friends for anything I might have done to hurt them, give a lot to charity, and pray to God with all of my heart to register me and my family in the Book of Life. It was during *Rosh Hashanah* that my personal relationship with God really developed because I would spend the whole holiday telling Him all of the things I wanted Him to grant me for the upcoming year — from good health to a new

Nintendo game (I was a child, after all!). When the holiday of *Rosh Hashanah* ended, I truly looked at God as my loving Father. I always left synagogue on this holy day with a feeling of peace and joy.

Now that I am older, I no longer pray for the same things that I did when I was young, yet that emotional attachment to God and the heartfelt prayers still envelop me from the moment *Rosh Hashanah* begins. I still call friends and loved ones before the holiday and share memories of the previous year in tears and laughter. The prayers sung in synagogue over *Rosh Hashanah* still move my soul. I have realized that each year I grow a little closer to God and a bit more faithful. The older I get and the more experiences I have, the more awed I am by His greatness.

My New Year's resolution is to include God in everything, and thank Him daily for the wonders He performs.

FIDF Bar Mitzvah celebration (FIDF)

GOING DEEPER FOR CHRISTIANS

What resolution might you make going forward from this day? How can you include God in your daily routine? What inspires you about God's greatness?

Read also:

• Luke 1:46–55

• Ephesians 1:18–20; 3:14–19

• Hebrews 12:28–29

MARKING OUR HOLIEST DAY OF THE YEAR

> "THIS IS TO BE A LASTING ORDINANCE FOR YOU: ON THE TENTH DAY OF THE SEVENTH MONTH YOU MUST DENY YOURSELVES AND NOT DO ANY WORK — WHETHER NATIVE-BORN OR A FOREIGNER RESIDING AMONG YOU — BECAUSE ON THIS DAY ATONEMENT WILL BE MADE FOR YOU, TO CLEANSE YOU. THEN, BEFORE THE LORD, YOU WILL BE CLEAN FROM ALL YOUR SINS."
>
> — LEVITICUS 16:29–30

Yom Kippur is one of the most intense and meaningful days on the Jewish calendar, and it holds special significance for me when I observe it in Israel. It is only on this special day that the busy main streets in Israel are suddenly quiet, downtown shops are closed, and even the most secular

Bnei Menashe man in prayer shawl (Karen Sandvick)

people can be seen entering the synagogues to pray. In Israel on this day, all of the Jewish people are united in our repentance and prayer for God to seal His nation and the entire world in the Book of Life.

The fast day of *Yom Kippur* lasts for 25 hours and enables us to enter God's chambers through pure and heartfelt prayer. The people of Israel wear white clothing and cloth shoes to represent the purity of angels and invoke God's compassion as He seals us in the Book of Life or the Book of Death for the upcoming year. *Yom Kippur* is the one sacred holiday without a festive meal or special songs of celebration; the day is focused solely on prayer and connecting to God.

Throughout the year I walk the streets of Israel and feel proud to call this land home, but on *Yom Kippur* my heart soars with a special burning love for all of Israel's people for appreciating the holiest day of the year and giving it the respect it deserves.

On this special day in Israel, nonobservant Jews are suddenly seen with religious skull caps on their heads and immersed in tearful prayers to their Creator; children who are too young to fast refrain from eating sugary snacks in honor of God's holy day; elderly immigrants cry out in thanks to God for gathering them home to the Holy Land in fulfillment of biblical prophecy.

Appropriately, it is not only happy times that we recollect on *Yom Kippur* but the hard times as well. It is an emotional day when loved ones mourn for those lost the previous year, and hold on to their faith that the upcoming year will be brighter. All of Israel somberly remembers the victims of terror who were brutally taken from us and desperately prays for the New Year to bring peace. We all stand united in each person's pain and unified in our prayers.

Celebrating the Day of Awe here in the Holy Land is truly inspiring. After the ram's horn is blown representing the end of *Yom Kippur*, I always emerge from the holiday feeling renewed, cleansed, and hopeful for the coming year. After a full day of conversing with God through prayer, meditation, and fasting, and seeing all of Israel engage in the same sincere repentance, it is clear to me that the day when the "*wolf will live with the lamb*" (Isaiah 11:6) is coming soon.

GOING DEEPER FOR CHRISTIANS

What lessons for repenting and coming before God do you glean from the traditions of *Yom Kippur*? How do you prepare for coming before God and asking forgiveness?

Read also:

• Romans 3:25–26

• Hebrews 7:26–27; 9:11–12

• 1 John 2:1–3

YOM KIPPUR: GOD'S WAKE-UP CALL

> "THE LORD IS NEAR TO ALL WHO CALL ON HIM, TO ALL WHO CALL ON HIM IN TRUTH. HE FULFILLS THE DESIRES OF THOSE WHO FEAR HIM; HE HEARS THEIR CRY AND SAVES THEM."
>
> — PSALM 145:18–19

It felt like angels were walking the streets of Jerusalem as residents made their way to Temple on *Yom Kippur*, dressed all in white to represent the spiritual state we all aspire to during this very holy day. Nearly every Jewish person in Israel attended Temple from morning until night. There were no cars on the streets, so children frolicked and played while parents watched from the windows of the synagogue.

Like any democracy, Israel is home to people of all levels of religious observance and widely varying political opinions. But *Yom Kippur* is the holiday that brings us all together. It is the one day a year when we put aside our differences and pray to God to grant us life, safety, health, prosperity, and happiness for the upcoming year. Although

Young woman with Scripture at Western Wall (Debbi Cooper)

each person makes his or her own personal appeal to God on *Yom Kippur*, I truly believe it is the intensity of the community coming together that touches the angels in heaven. On this day we know we are one because we are all God's children.

For me, *Yom Kippur* is a wake-up call for change. The world faces many problems, but *Yom Kippur* reminds me that all change must start within each person's heart and home. Although we may not be directly involved in high-level peace talks or economic debates, we are not powerless when it comes to these issues. In fact, we have the greatest weapon of all for change: prayer. I find that when I really pray with all my heart and cry out to God like I do each year on *Yom Kippur*, I see a direct change for good in my life. Seeing God at work in my life gives me confidence that I can change the world for the better.

All of us at one time have struggled with the question: Can I, one person, change the whole world? We all have a burning desire to leave the world a better place for our children and grandchildren. *Yom Kippur* is the day when God tells us, His children, that all we need to do is to approach Him with a humble and grateful heart and ask for the things we need, and He will do the rest.

Although *Yom Kippur* is a one-day observance for Jews, our prayers from those 24 hours follow us throughout the year. They are the voice in our ears asking us if each decision we make will bring us closer to or push us farther from God. *Yom Kippur* renews our resolve to listen to what God is telling us and to institute real change within ourselves, our families, and the world. If we all become conscious of the fact that God is speaking every second and that all He wants us to do is listen, I know that by next *Yom Kippur* we will be seeing happier, more hopeful times in our world.

GOING DEEPER FOR CHRISTIANS

What one thing would you most like to change in your life? In your community? In the world? What one step can you take today to begin that change?

Read also:

• Luke 18:1–8

• Ephesians 6:18

• Colossians 4:2–3

• 1 Thessalonians 5:17

• James 5:16b

EXPERIENCING GOD'S PRESENCE AT *SUKKOT*

> "LORD, I LOVE THE
> HOUSE WHERE YOU
> LIVE, THE PLACE
> WHERE YOUR
> GLORY DWELLS."
>
> — PSALM 26:8

The holiday of *Sukkot* is truly one of my favorite times of the year. I love building the *sukkah* (the outdoor hut that resembles the booths in which Israelites lived in the desert during their exile in biblical times) and making it my home for the seven days of the holiday. Together with my family and lots of guests, we eat meals in our *sukkah*, study *Torah*, sing, and dance. Because of the commandment to make the *sukkah* into a temporary house for seven days, my husband even sleeps there!

The walls of our *sukkah* are covered in decorations that my children made in school, and the roof is composed of special palm branches — *schach*, as they are called in Hebrew — that allow us to see the stars through the roof. It truly feels like an ancient home.

When I am sitting in my *sukkah* and hear my neighbors singing their praises to God in the *sukkah* next door, I look up to the heavens and thank Him for giving us the Jewish homeland. Only in Israel do all households — as well as businesses and even government buildings — build *sukkot* (the plural form of *sukkah*). Every *sukkah* has at least three walls built, and often people don't even add a fourth wall, just to show passersby that they are welcome to come in.

Tradition holds that on each day of *Sukkot* a different biblical forefather comes to visit the *sukkah* as a guest of honor — Abraham, Isaac, Jacob,

Moses, Aaron, David, and Solomon are all present. As I was building my *sukkah* this year, I realized the message that this tradition is trying to impart to us: If we build our house upon a holy foundation with godly intentions, God's presence will dwell there.

The *sukkah* is truly the merging of heaven and earth. We create a holy structure to protect and surround us, just as the cloud of glory protected the Israelites while they wandered in the desert. Though it's a simple structure, I think of it as being a temple, just like the Temple that stood in Jerusalem and will one day stand again as a resting place for God's glory. So too, when we build the *sukkah* as the *Torah* commands and fill it with holiness, God's glory rests within it.

A modern-day sukkah

Sukkot serves as a reminder of days past as well of what is to come. Just as the Jews witnessed God's miraculous salvation when we were taken out of Egypt and brought to Israel, so too, will we witness a new reality when the Messiah comes and spreads peace and love throughout the world. The holiday of *Sukkot* is a taste of what this will feel like, and I cherish every moment of this seven-day holiday that God gave us as a blessed gift.

GOING DEEPER FOR CHRISTIANS

Where do you feel God's presence in a special way? What do you do to connect with God?

Read also:

• John 1:14

• 1 Corinthians 3:16

• Ephesians 2:21–22

• 2 Peter 3:13

A SEASON OF LIGHT

"THE LORD IS MY

LIGHT AND MY

SALVATION—

WHOM SHALL

I FEAR?

THE LORD IS THE

STRONGHOLD

OF MY LIFE—

OF WHOM SHALL

I BE AFRAID?"

— PSALM 27:1

I love holidays, especially *Hanukkah*. The candles that burn in our house for eight days spread holiness to my surroundings. I feel the divine joy of fulfilling the *mitzvah* (biblical commandment) of lighting the menorah and remembering the miracle of one tiny jar of oil that maintained the light of the menorah in the ancient Jerusalem Temple for eight days straight. Whenever I light the *Hanukkah* candles and say the blessing, I pray to God that my generation will also witness godly miracles that strengthen our faith.

    Hanukkah is a time of happiness. For the entire eight days of the holiday, the country of Israel holds one big party to celebrate the miracles God performed in our very own homeland. We place our menorah outside our door, and around sunset when we are commanded to light the *Hanukkah* candles my family huddles together, sings traditional songs, and opens presents. Over the course of the holiday, it is tradition to eat lots of deep-fried food, since the miracle we are

Hanukkah *treats at Jerusalem's Mahane Yehuda market*
(ISRANET)

38

celebrating revolves around a jar of oil. Special treats are served in every Israeli store, and deep-fried donuts, called *sufganiyot*, are consumed by all. Eating the sweet and delicious food just adds to the joys of *Hanukkah*!

I feel so blessed to be able to visit the Western Wall on *Hanukkah* and stand at the very spot where the *Hanukkah* miracle took place. I always pray that the Temple should once again stand in Jerusalem, and the menorah should shine the light of peace and holiness to the world. As I watch thousands of people flock to Jerusalem over the holiday, it reminds me of how it will be when Messiah arrives; Jerusalem will be the center of the world.

I love how *Hanukkah* is called the "Festival of Lights." To me, candles represent holiness, godliness, and divinity. They shine light on the physical world, just as the Bible shines light on the spiritual world. *Hanukkah* is the holiday that celebrates and recognizes how God is involved in our daily lives and comes to our aid when we call on Him.

Psalm 27 says, "*The LORD is my light and my salvation — whom shall I fear? The LORD is the stronghold of my life — of whom shall I be afraid?*" I know that the *Hanukkah* candles hold a glimpse of God's light. My prayer this *Hanukkah* is that we always remember to trust only in God and fear nothing — because He is in control.

GOING DEEPER FOR CHRISTIANS

Share with your friends or family a time when you have felt God's light shining on you. How has God been your "light and salvation"?

Read also:

• Matthew 4:16; 5:14–15

• John 1:4–9; 3:20–21; 8:12

• 2 Corinthians 4:6

• Ephesians 5:8–9

• 1 Peter 2:9

DAILY LIVING

I feel so blessed to live in the Holy Land, where biblical prophecy is fulfilled before my eyes and ancient biblical stories come alive. Life in Israel has many trials and tribulations due to the unstable political reality, yet the beauty of the people, culture, and land shine through all these hardships, making Israel the best place in the world to live. Each time I leave my house, I know that a new adventure to strengthen my faith awaits me.

The unexpected has somehow become the assumed in Israel — whether it's meeting a holy person on a bus ride, driving down main streets named after biblical figures, or touring ancient holy sites that are blocks away from my house. Daily life in Israel is anything but ordinary.

Walk with me through my extraordinary days in Israel, as you read the section on *Daily Living* in the Holy Land. ∎

COMING HOME

Living in Jerusalem for the past seven years has been the best experience of my life. I remember stepping off the plane in the Holy Land for the first time and feeling a chill when the pilot looked at me and said, "Welcome home." After I exited the plane, I kneeled down to kiss the ground, and the promise that God made to Abraham repeated in my head: "*I will make your descendants as numerous as the stars in the sky and will give them all these lands, and through your offspring all nations on earth will be blessed*" (Genesis 26:4).

I can still feel the excitement and newness that I felt on the drive from the Tel Aviv airport to my new home in Jerusalem. Every flower had colors more vibrant then I have ever seen before, the mountains were glittering green, the sky looked as blue as the ocean, and the air was fresh and warm. I felt God welcoming me to His homeland and smiling at my return.

A mother and her children in Jerusalem
(Debbi Cooper)

For the first few months of living in Jerusalem, every day I left my house to walk along the ancient cobblestone paths in the Old City, I envisioned walking in the footsteps of the prophets. Looking into the mountains surrounding Jerusalem, I imagined King David hiding out and singing psalms. Although the holy biblical figures that we study daily lived so many generations ago, somehow in Jerusalem they still seem very present.

The amazing balance of ancient and modern makes Jerusalem like no other city on earth. Modern Jerusalem is a thriving, productive, gentrified city with much to offer in every area. Shopping malls and restaurants, as well as ancient synagogues and churches, all lie nestled within Jerusalem's Old City walls, which are thousands of years old.

To think about how much this small country has accomplished in such a short period of time is astonishing, and can be fully credited to the Jewish people's hard work and God's strength. Looking out at my beautiful city of Jerusalem, I am constantly reminded of the prayer that Jews around the world have raised to God through our 2,000 years of exile: "O God, build up Jerusalem, the Holy City, speedily in our days."

Seven years after settling in the Promised Land, the newness and excitement of living in Jerusalem has calmed down a bit. I am used to seeing people stop in the middle of the highway to recite their afternoon prayers and watching little children recite Bible verses by heart. I no longer pause in wonder at the dazzling colors of the flowers, the ancient cobblestone streets, or the prophets' names on street signs.

But like old and cherished friends, these things are no less dear to me because they are familiar. They have become part of my everyday life here in the Holy City, my home.

GOING DEEPER FOR CHRISTIANS

When you think of Jerusalem, what images come to mind? What does it mean to you that this is God's Holy City?

Read also:

• Matthew 5:34–35

• Luke 13:34

• Hebrews 12:22–23

• Revelation 3:12; 21:2

A STATEMENT OF FAITH

"HOW GOOD AND PLEASANT IT IS WHEN GOD'S PEOPLE LIVE TOGETHER IN UNITY!"

— PSALM 133:1

Often *The Fellowship*'s Christian supporters ask me what Jews believe. Well, since *The Fellowship* is all about building bridges between these two great religions, today I want to share with you a bit about my faith.

I am an Orthodox Jew who loves the Bible, God, and all of His children. I live my life in a way that I believe will make God happy, and I use the Bible as my instruction book. My feelings of accomplishment lay in honoring the Sabbath, keeping the biblical laws regarding kosher living, and moving to the Holy Land. Every day I strive to live by His word.

I study the Psalms and find the words to be beautiful and inspiring. One of my favorite verses is Psalm 133:1: "*How good and pleasant it is when God's people live together in unity!*" It is clear to me that the bridge-building work of

Yael Eckstein at the Western Wall (Debbi Cooper)

44

the *International Fellowship of Christians and Jews* fulfills that psalm and brings joy to our Lord.

Christians and Jews have many shared foundational values, and when we focus on the points that bring us together — such as love for God, studying and obeying His word, support for Israel, emphasis on prayer and charity, belief in Judeo-Christian values — we are bettering the world and giving honor to our Creator.

In the years since my father, Rabbi Eckstein, founded *The Fellowship*, we have made great strides for Jewish and Christian communities, as well as for the world, in honoring the biblical commandment to "*love your neighbor as yourself*" (Leviticus 19:18). Together, Christians and Jews have saved hundreds of thousands of impoverished lives and transformed them into independent individuals. And Christians and Jews continue to fulfill biblical prophecy by bringing the Jewish people home to Israel from the four corners of the earth, just as Isaiah prophesized!

I pray that we all will continuously grow closer to God and have the strength and vision to shine the light of His holiness to the world. Amen!

GOING DEEPER FOR CHRISTIANS

With your family or friends, complete this sentence: "I strive to honor God by

_____."

Read also:

• Ephesians 4:21–24

• Colossians 3:12

• 1 Thessalonians 4:11–12

• 1 Peter 1:5

BIRTH & REDEMPTION IN THE HOLY CITY

"THE SALVATION OF THE RIGHTEOUS COMES FROM THE LORD; HE IS THEIR STRONGHOLD IN TIME OF TROUBLE."

— PSALM 37:39

Throughout the pregnancy of my second child, I combed the Bible for verses pertaining to childbirth. While I found many with beautiful insights into the meaning of life and of motherhood, none were the exact verse that could carry me through the pain of childbirth. Now, I see that God was just waiting for the right time to reveal the words that would strengthen me when I needed it most.

While I was preparing to bring a new life into the world, a dear friend of mine, Shira, was fighting a painful battle with cancer. Shira was the most beautiful, smart, courageous, and spiritually wise person I have ever met. She drew life from God's word and from the land of Israel the way that a plant draws life from water and the sun. Shira was a mother, wife, daughter, sister, and friend who inspired every person she met. Throughout her struggle, her face was never without a smile, and her hands were never without her prayer book. Her words were always positive, despite the pain she was forced to endure at the young age of 25. This was

(Debbi Cooper)

true until she drew her last breath just a month before my son was born.

Shira was in pain nearly every moment of the day, and yet she held firmly to the Jewish teaching that "God brings redemption in the blink of an eye." During

46

Shira's illness, this biblical thought was constantly on her lips. The knowledge that God is in control and could — in the blink of an eye — change her pain into relief enabled her to endure. Each time her pain eased, she praised God for redeeming her from the suffering she knew all too well, even if it was only for a moment.

During my labor, I followed Shira's example. Whenever the pain seemed unbearable, I remembered that "God brings redemption in the blink of an eye." I confidently repeated this in my mind and, before I knew it, the pain had subsided. Instead of focusing on the pain of the contractions, I used the contractions as a new opportunity to strengthen my faith.

When the nurse told my husband and me that our baby would be born soon, we immediately took out our book of Psalms and sang songs of praise to God. We wanted these ancient and immortal words to be the first ones our child heard as he came into the world.

Ten minutes after the nurse came in, at 9:30 a.m. on a magical *Shabbat* morning in the Holy City of Jerusalem, our healthy, beautiful baby boy was born. My husband and I looked at each other with tears streaming down our faces. We didn't need to say a word, because we both knew in our hearts that we were thinking the same thing: What a life-changing, beautiful, and redemptive birth we had just experienced!

After our son's birth, I thanked God for His grace and for Shira, who had taught me so much. From her I learned that, although there are great hardships in the world, God brings comfort. If we place our full trust and hope in Him, He can give us the ability to endure those hardships.

GOING DEEPER FOR CHRISTIANS

During difficult times, where do you find strength? What lesson of hope have you found during a difficult circumstance?

Read also:

• Luke 1:68–69; 2:29–31

• Acts 4:12

• Romans 1:16

• Revelation 7:10

HOLY MOMENTS FROM ISRAEL

> "FOR YOU ARE A
> PEOPLE HOLY TO
> THE LORD YOUR
> GOD. THE LORD
> YOUR GOD HAS
> CHOSEN YOU
> OUT OF ALL THE
> PEOPLES ON THE
> FACE OF THE EARTH
> TO BE HIS PEOPLE,
> HIS TREASURED
> POSSESSION."
>
> — DEUTERONOMY 7:6

It was a typical day in Jerusalem, and yet magical — a day that reminded me that a spark of godliness dwells in everything in the Holy City, if I'll just have the eyes to see it.

After living here for nearly seven years, I have come to realize there is nothing ordinary about the people or events in this sanctified city. Riding on the bus to a nearby playground with my daughter last week, I became aware of my divine surroundings. An elderly immigrant woman was reading her book of Psalms intently. A child was telling his mother about the Bible lessons he had learned in school. The names I overheard in conversations around me were all biblical: Joshua, Moses, Isaiah, Aaron. I treasure these typical, everyday moments in Israel. I sat in my seat amazed at how riding the local bus in Jerusalem could bring me closer to God!

When we arrived at our destination, I noticed that the playground supervisor sported many earrings, wore unorthodox clothing, and had dyed hair. I didn't expect her to be religious, but I was pleasantly surprised when I saw her leave her post to say the traditional Jewish afternoon prayers in a quiet space nearby.

People entering the playground found this woman completely immersed in intense prayer to God. As she prayed she covered her eyes, absorbed in the ancient words she was reciting. I left the playground inspired and powerfully reminded never to judge a book by its cover. I thought of the biblical verse

Mother with child in Jerusalem (Debbi Cooper)

that tells us to "*love your neighbor as yourself*" (Leviticus 19:18), and made a vow to try harder to enact this teaching in my own life.

That evening, I attended my best friend's wedding in the mountains of Judah. The ceremony took place in the same spot where the first Jewish marriage document ever was found, dating from thousands of years ago. I looked over at my husband and had tears in my eyes when I explained to him the awe I felt when I realized that everything we do in Israel is grounded in our biblical heritage and history.

I feel so blessed to live in Jerusalem, where we breathe the air of redemption and create a holy space for God to dwell in this world. And I thank Him every day for giving us friends around the world who support us in good times and bad.

GOING DEEPER FOR CHRISTIANS

What does it mean to you to be considered one of God's holy people? How does that knowledge play out in your life?

Read also:

• Acts 26:18

• 1 Peter 2:5, 9

• Revelation 1:6

LOVE YOUR NEIGHBOR

> "DO NOT SEEK
> REVENGE OR BEAR
> A GRUDGE AGAINST
> ANYONE AMONG
> YOUR PEOPLE,
> BUT LOVE
> YOUR NEIGHBOR
> AS YOURSELF.
> I AM THE LORD."
>
> — LEVITICUS 19:18

The God-given commandment to *"love your neighbor as yourself"* is shown in every area of life in Israel. The unity, harmony, and mutual support fostered by those biblical words are what keep our spirits high in the face of the often bleak reality of our situation.

Despite the isolation that Israel has been pushed into by so many in the international community, the people of Israel never feel alone. We have one another, we have God, and we have our faithful Christian supporters, which gives us the strength and confidence

Recipient of Fellowship *support thanks Yael Eckstein*
(IFCJ)

to go on. In both the mundane and the dramatic moments of our lives, the Israeli people provide each other with a strong network of support, encouragement, and hope.

I remember after I gave birth to both of my children, people in my community — many of whom I did not even know — cooked meals for my family on a daily basis for nearly a month and delivered them to my home. Another time, when I was walking in the pouring rain without an umbrella, a woman pulled over in her car and insisted on driving me home. In Israel, a mugging occurring on the street with no one intervening — as happens, sadly, elsewhere — is unthinkable. If an elderly person falls on the street, you can count on people rushing to help her up. Here in Israel, we are brothers and sisters — and our actions toward one another reveal that.

This kinship shows through in the immediate moments after a terror attack. Instead of people running away from the chaos and carnage, people run from all directions toward it. People seem unconcerned for their own safety and want only to help the wounded, who are treated by passersby as their own family. Strangers sit with the wounded, comforting them and desperately trying to help. Almost anyone would risk his life to save a victim of terror. When one person hurts, the entire country feels his pain.

Despite the ongoing terror and the media's bleak predictions about our future, the nation of Israel is strong and confident. We have each other, we have friends like you, and we have God. Despite the international isolation, we know that we are never really alone.

GOING DEEPER FOR CHRISTIANS

As you go through your day, look for opportunities to help those around you. Share a word of encouragement with someone who is hurting; visit someone who is sick or housebound; help an elderly neighbor with a household task.

Read also:

• Mark 12:30–32

• Galatians 5:14

• James 2:8

GOD'S GRACE AMID THE TERROR

"I KNOW THAT YOU CAN DO ALL THINGS; NO PURPOSE OF YOURS CAN BE THWARTED."

— JOB 42:2

I woke up this morning to news that Israel has declared a unilateral cease-fire in the Hamas-controlled Gaza Strip. Personally, I have mixed feelings about a cease-fire. But what really touched me was how the Israeli government implemented the decision. Instead of convening the security cabinet on Friday, the Jewish Sabbath, they waited until sundown on Saturday in order to make this crucial decision after God's commanded day of rest had concluded.

Throughout the three-week war in Gaza, we have seen miracles that have assured us that God is with the Jewish people in this battle for Israel's survival. The number of casualties has remained relatively low. And in the seven years that Hamas has fired over 7,000 rockets at Israel's southern towns, most of them have landed in open fields and streets. Again, there is no natural explanation for this other than God's grace. The Jewish people are the apple of God's eye, and we see how important we are to Him by the cloud of glory with which He surrounds us. That is why I was so proud when my country convened the security cabinet after the Jewish Sabbath had ended, in order to show proper respect, thanks, and recognition to God after the wonders that He has performed for His nation.

The war in Gaza began during *Hanukkah*, which everyone knows as the holiday of miracles — the small jar of olive oil that should have lasted only one day burned for eight days, and the small number of Jews led by the Maccabees who prevailed against the far greater number of soldiers of the Greeks. The spirit of *Hanukkah* was carried on throughout the war in Gaza, and God sent both open and hidden miracles to inspire, encourage, and protect His nation during this time of war.

The soldiers returning from Gaza have publicly recounted many miracle stories, yet one story stood out above the rest. A group of soldiers was going house to house in Gaza looking for terrorists. As they entered one house, an old lady approached and told them that the house was booby-trapped and that they should run out immediately. They complied, and 30 seconds later the house exploded. The soldiers went to the next house, where the same woman approached and told them to run. Thirty seconds later, the house exploded. She then led them to a house where she said high-ranking terrorists were hiding, and in fact, she was correct.

When the soldiers asked the old lady how she knew all of these things, she

Rockets being fired from Gaza (ISRANET)

simply answered that she is Rachel, our biblical matriarch, sent to watch out for the soldiers. She then walked away and was never seen again. According to many different accounts from the soldiers this story is true, yet whether you choose to believe it or not, there is a lesson to be learned: When we put our faith in God, He will reveal Himself.

We Israelis have been trained to believe in miracles. Together we stand firm in our desire for peace and will continue to take every opportunity to attain it. We know that through prayer and faithfulness to God, nothing is impossible — even peace in the Holy Land.

GOING DEEPER FOR CHRISTIANS

When you hear of a miracle occurring in someone's life, what is your initial reaction? Why is it hard for people to believe that God still works miracles for His people? When has God performed a miracle for you?

Read also:

• Matthew 17:20

• Mark 10:27; 14:36

THE MOST HOLY SITE

> "ONE THING
> I ASK FROM
> THE LORD, THIS
> ONLY DO I SEEK:
> THAT I MAY DWELL
> IN THE HOUSE
> OF THE LORD ALL
> THE DAYS OF
> MY LIFE, TO GAZE
> ON THE BEAUTY
> OF THE LORD
> AND TO SEEK HIM
> IN HIS TEMPLE."
>
> — PSALM 27:4

The Western Wall, which stands in the Old City of Jerusalem, is considered the holiest site in Judaism. It is the only wall from the Second Temple period still standing, and Jews all over the world direct their hearts and prayers toward this remnant of the biblical past. Everyone who prays toward this spot has faith that

The Western Wall (IFCJ)

God's special dwelling place is a spiritual one, and therefore, just because the structure of the ancient Temple was destroyed, His strong presence remains where the Temple once stood, even though the physical Temple does not.

When I made *aliyah* (immigrated to Israel) seven years ago from America, my first stop on the way to my new home in Jerusalem was the Western Wall. To me, the Wall represents not just every Jew's yearning to return to Israel, but also their right to return to Israel. Even during the many years of the Jews' exile from their biblical homeland, the Western Wall remained our most visible "mark" on the city. The Jewish claim to Jerusalem was never forgotten nor disputed, because we always had our ancestors' handiwork present: the lone remaining wall of the Temple.

Jewish tradition holds that the Western Wall of the Temple was built through the donations of the poor. God realized what a sacrifice those families made in order to give the little money that they could to build His dwelling, so He did not let their wall burn with the rest of Jerusalem. Rather, He kept it standing strong to this day to show the world that God cares for the poor.

When I am standing next to the Wall, I envision the Temple work being performed as it was in days of old. Sometimes, if I close my eyes, I can almost smell the scent of the sacrifices that were offered in that very spot thousands of years ago by King Solomon, and taste the tears of the thousands of people who come to the Wall daily, praying and begging God for divine guidance and help.

I believe that prayers said at the Wall go directly up to heaven. This was revealed to me when I went to the Wall praying for a healthy child. Nine months later, I found myself standing at that very same spot with my beautiful new daughter. The wonders that God performs daily keep me in awe.

I know with all my heart that every prayer from all over the world is heard. Yet to pray in the spot where both Temples once stood adds certain intensity to the prayer. I think of the Western Wall as an ancient gateway to heaven. What a privilege it is to live just five minutes away from this ancient and holy place!

GOING DEEPER FOR CHRISTIANS

According to Christian beliefs and Scripture, the body is God's temple now. In what ways do you see your body as God's temple? How does that impact how you care for your body?

Read also:

• Matthew 12:6

• Mark 13:1–2

• John 2:19–21

• 1 Corinthians 3:16–17; 6:19

• 2 Corinthians 6:16

THE BLESSINGS OF THE SABBATH

I have celebrated the *Shabbat* (the Sabbath) in many places around the world. Whether I'm in Israel, Chicago, Florida, Nashville, Russia, or Ethiopia, when the sun begins to set on Friday — marking the beginning of the seventh day of the week — I light the *Shabbat* candles and begin my day of rest, just as the Bible commands. This God-ordained weekly celebration fills me with a comforting feeling of order and holiness.

My entire schedule is planned around the *Shabbat*, which is worth more to me than any worldly possession. What a beautiful gift to be biblically commanded one day a week to put aside all work and stress, and to focus on God and my family — the two most important priorities in my life!

In my home, *Shabbat* is a time of singing, dancing, praying, and fellowship. The doors to the house are left open, and my husband and I welcome guests to take part in our *Shabbat* meals, which are filled with laughter and joy. My children wait anxiously

Looking at Mt. Precipice from Nazareth Village synagogue
(IFCJ)

by the door for our guests to arrive, and plan games to play with the other kids. While waiting, they sing special songs and help me set the *Shabbat* table, which is always full of their favorite food and beautiful flowers.

Shabbat is a time my husband and I use to bless our children and instill in them the values that we hold dear. We make sure there's plenty of opportunity for fun and games to make celebrating the *Shabbat* a positive experience for them. Once they see how enjoyable it is to celebrate the *Shabbat*, they develop a greater love and appreciation for all of God's commandments. It is a powerful and inspiring thing to know that your children are in love with the Lord!

Looking around the world, it seems a day of rest is what many people are longing for. We're stressed out from long hours at work, schedules that are too full, and the unending noise of phone calls, e-mails, and text messages. Nearly everyone could benefit from one day a week to simply revel in God's creation without the pressures of the outside world. God gave us the *Shabbat* because He is a God of kindness and wants us to have a chance to relax and focus on faith, prayer, and family — and Himself! Turning off all cell phones, computers, and televisions for *Shabbat* is not a restriction — it's a freeing experience.

The comfort that I find in God and the Bible culminates on the *Shabbat*, when I truly feel wrapped in His glory. *Shabbat* is one effective way to stay strong in our values and preserve the holiness of the Bible, while ultimately paving the path to a bright and peaceful future for our children and generations to come.

GOING DEEPER FOR CHRISTIANS

In what ways do you set aside time on a weekly basis to honor and worship God? What other steps might you take to ensure that Sunday is a day of rest for you?

Read also:

• Matthew 12:1–8

• Mark 2:27–28

• Hebrews 4:9–11

"So Ephron's field in Machpelah near Mamre — both the field and the cave in it, and all the trees within the borders of the field — was deeded to Abraham as his property in the presence of all the Hittites who had come to the gate of the city. Afterward Abraham buried his wife Sarah in the cave in the field of Machpelah near Mamre (which is at Hebron) in the land of Canaan."

— Genesis 23:17–19

Visit to the Tomb of the Patriarchs

I was visiting the holy city of Hebron for the first time, and admittedly, it was a bit nerve-wracking. In order to get to this biblical city, which houses the Tomb of the Patriarchs, I had to take a bulletproof car deep into disputed West Bank territory — biblical Judea and Samaria. Reciting a heartfelt prayer for safety, I began my journey and placed my complete trust in God.

As I entered the West Bank, I felt the strong presence of Israeli soldiers protecting the road and stopping suspicious cars. Beyond the road were beautiful mountains and small homes surrounded by herds of goats and cattle. The Israeli flags waving strong and proud from Jewish homes nestled in the hills brought a smile to my face. Settling in the Holy Land is the dream that the Jewish people have been praying throughout our 2,000 years of exile, and how awesome to see biblical prophecy fulfilled before my eyes!

Although Hebron in this way felt ordinary, it is in fact an extraordinary place. Just a two-minute drive away from the last home in the town stands the Tomb of the Patriarchs, where many of the Jewish patriarchs and matriarchs are buried.

The tomb was awe-inspiring. As I stood next to the grave of Abraham, I felt like the most fortunate person in the world to have the privilege of praying at this ancient, biblical, holy site. I recited some psalms next to Sarah's grave, then went on to Jacob's resting place. I remained at the tomb for over an hour, praying for everyone and everything that entered my heart.

I prayed and asked God for peace in Israel, America, and the entire world.
As I turned to leave, I kissed the tomb, and an overwhelming feeling of
divine love entered my soul.

Israeli flag over settlement (IFCJ)

Now, a few days later, I
still feel God's presence close
to my heart, and I know that I
am changed forever. That is the
beauty of visiting holy sites:
Their influence remains with
you eternally.

I feel so blessed to live in the
Holy Land, where biblical sites
are located around every corner
and God's word can be heard
from the top of every mountain. I look forward to the day when true peace
will come, and driving to and from Hebron will no longer be dangerous —
the miraculous day spoken of in Scripture when "*the wolf will live with the
lamb, the leopard will lie down with the goat, the calf and the lion and the
yearling together; and a little child will lead them*" (Isaiah 11:6).

GOING DEEPER FOR CHRISTIANS

When you consider the
current situation in the
world, what discourages
you? What brings you hope?

Read also:

• Luke 2:14

• John 14:27; 16:33

• Romans 5:1–2; 14:17–19

• 1 Corinthians 14:33

• Colossians 3:15

FROM FEAR TO FAITH

Several years ago, the Israeli government instructed all its citizens to equip their houses with gas masks. Israelis heeded this call because we all take seriously the threat from our enemies who espouse Israel's demise. Although this is a potentially fearful situation, it is beautiful to see how faith and the Bible keep us hopeful and steadfast. God's word gives us life and speaks louder than the threatening words of a terrorist.

Yet when I opened my family's box of gas masks, my initial feeling was fear. I recalled stories from the Second Lebanon War of 2006, when families were cramped in their bomb shelters with crying children. I pictured the president of Iran speaking about his nuclear ambitions and the missiles that are already stationed in his country pointed toward Israel. I visualized a map of the region, with tiny Israel surrounded on all sides by her enemies. As my fear rose in my throat, I recalled the words of Psalm 127:1 — *"Unless the LORD watches over the city, the guards stand watch in vain"* — and I was filled with faith and peace.

Practically speaking, Israel's very existence seems unlikely. We are a country of more than seven million people, about three quarters of them Jews, surrounded by millions of Arabs, many of whom are deeply hostile to us. Yet we have survived for more than 60 years and are growing ever stronger. We have few natural resources, yet have produced great technological advances that benefit the entire world. Despite bleak projections for the future, we remain hopeful and faithful.

I believe that Israel's very existence proves to the world that God stands with us. Our improbable history and ability to beat the odds have taught me that if you build a foundation on faith, anything is possible. Although our enemies seem set on Israel's destruction, I have faith that day will never come because we have God to protect us. As Psalm 121:4 reassures us, *"he who watches over Israel will neither slumber nor sleep."*

Later, as I regarded the box of gas masks, my fear had abated. Although the prospect of war is frightening, Israel stands firm in the knowledge that *"the* LORD *Almighty is with us; the God of Jacob is our fortress"* (Psalm 46:7). Knowing that we have *Fellowship* supporters who have given generously to renovate bomb shelters and equip emergency clinics and hospitals in case of an attack is a great comfort as well. We have been assured that never again will the Jewish people stand alone, thanks to friends like you.

Young children taking cover after warning siren
(ISRANET)

GOING DEEPER FOR CHRISTIANS

Share a time and situation when faith replaced fear for you. In what ways have you experienced God's protection?

Read also:

• Luke 8:22–25

• Romans 8:15

• 1 Peter 2:13–14

• 1 John 4:18

SEEING THE DESERT BLOOM

"THE DESERT AND
THE PARCHED LAND
WILL BE GLAD;
THE WILDERNESS
WILL REJOICE AND
BLOSSOM. LIKE THE
CROCUS, IT WILL
BURST INTO BLOOM;
IT WILL REJOICE
GREATLY AND
SHOUT FOR JOY."

— ISAIAH 35:1–2a

The entire State of Israel now celebrates the Jewish Ethiopian holiday of *Sigd*. This occasion reminds me of how thankful to God I am for our amazing donors who have changed Jewish history as we know it. Thanks to their generous donations, the once-lost tribe of Dan is now living comfortably in the Holy Land, as prophesized in our holy book thousands of years ago.

Each time I hear about the story of *Sigd*, I get the chills anew. The Ethiopian Jews — while still exiled in rural Ethiopia — established this holiday to sanctify themselves for God and merit reunion with the Jewish people. As one Ethiopian father explained to me while hugging his little baby in his arms, "We would fast all day, then hike up to the highest mountain in Ethiopia, where the spiritual leader would pray to God that the Ethiopian Jews should be worthy to return to Zion." Looking at his son and wiping a tear from his eyes, he turned his face toward heaven. "God truly answers our prayers," he said. "My son was born three weeks ago in Jerusalem."

It never ceases to amaze me to realize we are truly living in

Ethiopians at transit camp waiting to make aliyah
(Debbi Cooper)

62

prophetic times. It's hard to imagine that the world was without the Jewish State of Israel for over 2,000 years. And now, just a few generations after my grandfather survived the Holocaust in Germany, I have two beautiful children born in the mountains of Jerusalem. It is this time in history that the prophets were referring to when they wrote about the Messiah's imminent arrival.

Although *Sigd* is a holiday that Ethiopian Jews have exclusively celebrated for centuries, it is a holiday that I relate to. When I consider my neighbors, my friends, even myself, I realize that nearly everyone was an immigrant. Since Israel's inception in 1948, Jews in Israel have gathered from Europe, America, Russia, Iran, and countless other countries of their birth. Uniting in Jerusalem is the answer to all of our prayers, because all of us were once strangers in a strange land. The holiday of *Sigd* commemorates the struggles we all went through to arrive in the Holy Land, and the love that God will always have for His children.

I feel so blessed to be living in the Holy Land. I thank God that when my children read the books of the prophets, they can literally see the holy words coming alive. Faith for them is not challenging or oppressive, but celebratory and beautiful. They will live out the words of the prophet Isaiah.

The Bible says that when the Jewish people return to Israel, they will witness "the desert bloom," and we have indeed seen this. Yet what is so amazing for me to see is how the State of Israel has made the Jewish people bloom as well into strong, confident, faithful servants of God who will love His land with all of their heart and soul.

GOING DEEPER FOR CHRISTIANS

In what ways has God kept His promises to you? Take a moment to thank God for what He has done for you.

Read also:

- Acts 3:22–33
- Romans 15:7–12
- 2 Corinthians 1:20

BUILDING A LEGACY

> "THE BLAMELESS
> SPEND THEIR DAYS
> UNDER THE LORD'S
> CARE, AND THEIR
> INHERITANCE WILL
> ENDURE FOREVER."
>
> — PSALM 37:18

I am constantly awed at how the biblical characters who lived so long ago give value and meaning to my life today. As I strive to mirror the attributes of our biblical ancestors who lived in a world very different from our own, I continue to learn from them. Their lives and experiences teach me that life is a gift and should be filled with unwavering holiness, charity, and kindness, irrespective of prevailing politics or society's pressures.

Moses filled an immoral, idol-worshiping world with a new system of morals and ethics when he brought the Ten Commandments down from Mount Sinai. He is a hero for leading the Israelites out of slavery and into the Promised Land and for relentlessly crying out to God on behalf of His children. His godly example and life lessons continue to impact God's people today. Moses lived 120 years, yet his legacy is immeasurable. Our biblical ancestors teach us that our impact upon the world can extend far beyond our lifespan.

The evidence of this fundamental truth is overwhelming. I think of Oskar Schindler, a German Catholic businessman, who rescued innocent Jews during the Holocaust, providing life to more than a thousand European Jews and their descendants. Philanthropist James A. de Rothschild financed the *Knesset* (Israel's parliament) building as a gift to the State of Israel; his legacy lives on in this amazing building that houses Israel's government — one of the few democracies in the Middle East. The more than 2,000 trees outside the Yad Vashem Holocaust Museum in Jerusalem are an enduring testimony to the heroic legacy of the "righteous Gentiles" who saved Jews during the Holocaust.

The Jewish people place a strong emphasis on moral achievement and charitable giving because we realize that their impact endures long after we are gone. When we die, we cannot take our career, bank account, or social standing along; only our righteous acts that God holds eternally sacred live on. The best way to ensure that we all leave an everlasting legacy is to begin building it now through acts of kindness and generosity.

Looking around the Jewish homeland, I know that it is thanks only to God's grace, hard work, and the generosity of Israel's friends that we have gotten this far. I trust that the Lord will continue to send us godly friends who will enable us to grow, flourish, and succeed.

GOING DEEPER FOR CHRISTIANS

What legacy would you like to leave behind for your children? For your friends? For your community?

Read also:

• Ephesians 1:13–15, 18

• Colossians 1:9–12

• Hebrews 9:15

FAITH AND COURAGE IN SDEROT

> "I LIFT UP MY
> EYES TO THE
> MOUNTAINS —
> WHERE DOES MY
> HELP COME FROM?
> MY HELP COMES
> FROM THE LORD,
> THE MAKER OF
> HEAVEN AND
> EARTH."
>
> — PSALM 121:1–2

During a recent visit to Sderot, an Israeli town that for years has been the target of Palestinian terrorist rockets fired from the nearby Gaza Strip, I must admit I was a little nervous. In recent months, rocket attacks have escalated, and terror is still a part of daily life.

When we got to Sderot, I was surprised to see it functioning like any other city. Mothers were walking their children to school, grocery-store owners were tending their shops, buses were making their rounds, and fathers were kissing their families as they drove off to work. I was awed and inspired that these people seemed to carry on normal lives despite being subjected to barrages of rockets for more than a decade.

Yet the reality that the people in Sderot live with on a daily basis soon became evident. At the local police station, a storeroom houses hundreds of spent shells from the lethal terrorist rockets that have fallen. "There have been days when these rockets would fall nonstop," the mayor told us. "If it weren't for the *Fellowship*-sponsored bomb shelters, I don't know what we would do. All of my citizens would be exposed, and we would be seeing many more casualties."

Driving around the city, there were other signs that life here is far from normal. In Sderot, there are bus stops that are also bomb shelters, children's parks with bomb-shelter slides and tunnels, windowless school buildings made out of pure concrete, and huge speakers at each street corner to sound

Spent rockets in Sderot (Debbi Cooper)

the "code red" siren when rockets are approaching.

If I lived here, I thought to myself, *I would be terrified to ever let my children leave the bomb shelter*. A 15-second warning of an impending rocket strike by a "code red" siren rarely provides enough time to find shelter, especially if you are walking on the street.

Yet, I noticed something else. Despite all they had been through, and the fact that rocket attacks have resumed and even escalated, the residents of Sderot whom I met seemed to have entrusted God with their homes, their children, their lives, and their futures. What an inspiration to see this level of faith from people who have been through so much!

GOING DEEPER FOR CHRISTIANS

What circumstances in your life right now cause you anxiety and fear? How do the words of Psalm 121 encourage you?

Read also:

• Matthew 6:25

• Philippians 4:6

• 1 Peter 5:7

SHINING IN A DARK WORLD

People sometimes ask me how I can raise my children in Israel, a country surrounded by enemies who promote terrorism, hate, and fear. My answer is simple: I am raising them in their true home, a place that teaches them to shine in our dark world.

I thought of this recently when I attended a large and moving event held by a righteous rabbi in memory of his father. In the dark of the night, Rabbi Ifergan threw thousands of candles into a burning fire to bring more godly light into the world in his father's honor. Watching this holy man perform this ancient ceremony with such love was inspiring.

I felt the warmth of the fire with not just my body but also my soul. I thought, *Just as a candle flame floats upwards yet is held down by the wick, we should always be reaching toward God while being grounded in this world to live His truth*. I felt a compelling responsibility to the world when I realized how one candle has the ability to light countless others.

The ceremony struck me deeply, and awakened my burning love for God, Israel, and all of His people. The sight of thousands of people standing in the night with the rabbi, singing psalms, clapping their hands, and reveling in holiness as if they were at the best concert in the world, was truly awe-inspiring.

The event was covered in all the newspapers the next morning. I am so happy that this holy country is captivated by saints, the Bible, and good deeds instead of just physical beauty or the latest fashion trends. The "superstars" in Israel include influential rabbis, major philanthropists, and heroic soldiers. Israelis cherish righteous actions, just as God does. I love the way His people here mirror His heart, and I love that my children witness that every day.

I also love how my children come home from school and speak about the founding fathers of this country as Abraham, Isaac, and Jacob, and I love seeing their excitement when an ancient artifact from the Temple period is unearthed just a few blocks from our house. I feel proud of the education they receive, because along with math, science, and biology, they are also required to memorize the names of major philanthropists and their contributions to Israeli society.

Israel may be surrounded by countries that breed terrorism and hate, but she steadfastly clings to her strong spiritual heritage and godly values. I am raising my children to be candles that will light the world with holiness and truth. We are blessed to live in a place that fans those flames to burn strong for Him.

GOING DEEPER FOR CHRISTIANS

In what ways are you a light to your family, your neighborhood, your community? What might you do to share your light with others?

Read also:

• Matthew 4:15–17

• John 1:1–9; 3:20–21; 8:12

• 2 Corinthians 4:5

• Ephesians 5:8

• Revelation 21:23–24

WHERE STRANGERS ARE FAMILY

> "THE FOREIGNER RESIDING AMONG YOU MUST BE TREATED AS YOUR NATIVE-BORN. LOVE THEM AS YOURSELF, FOR YOU WERE FOREIGNERS IN EGYPT. I AM THE LORD YOUR GOD."
>
> — LEVITICUS 19:34

As I was walking the sunny streets of Jerusalem with my father and daughter, we stopped a kind old woman to ask her where the nearest park was. She directed us to a park several blocks away and told us that my daughter would surely enjoy it. She continued on her way as we lagged a few steps behind, cherishing the picture of my little girl smelling the flowers then just coming into bloom.

In fact, we were enjoying the marvels of spring so much that we got lost. There was no one on the road whom we could ask for directions, so we continued on our way until we came to the garden of a house that was being tended by the same old lady. Feeling right at home like all Jerusalemites feel with one another, we entered and again asked her for directions. With a warm smile she told us how to get to the park, and then took my daughter's hand and led her to the garden's fish pond. I realized that the park would have to wait, because feeding fish is just too exciting for a two year old to pass up.

As we stood in the garden my father and I looked at each other and smiled. I knew that we were thinking the same thing: What a blessing to be raising a child in a country where she can be taught to trust strangers and turn to them for help. How beautiful it is that here in Jerusalem this old lady looks at my daughter as her own and seems to take joy just from watching her smile. My father summed up our feelings. "Only in the Holy Land," he said to me. "Only in Jerusalem would I trust a stranger with my precious granddaughter."

When we looked at the name on the elderly lady's mailbox, my father's face lit up. "Yael," he said to me, "I think this lady might be my great-aunt!" He rushed over to the fish pond and asked the woman if she was the sister of Aunt Leah, and she answered yes. Our "stranger" was a member of our family!

After hours of drinking coffee, playing in the garden, and catching up on family members, it was time for us to leave the home of the woman we now knew as Aunt Sarah. We entered her home as strangers but departed with hugs and kisses. Knowing we were blood relatives surely strengthened our bond, but even when we thought she was a stranger, we still had a feeling of genuine love and trust for her.

Here in Israel we Jews are unified by the knowledge that we are God's children who have been given the great privilege of finally living in the Holy Land.

(IFCJ)

GOING DEEPER FOR CHRISTIANS

Think of a time when a stranger reached out to you. How did that make you feel? How can you reach out to someone who is new to your neighborhood, workplace, or church?

Read also:

• Ephesians 2:19

• Hebrews 11:13; 13:2

• 3 John 1:5

SIRENS IN JERUSALEM

"INDEED, HE
WHO WATCHES
OVER ISRAEL WILL
NEITHER SLUMBER
NOR SLEEP."

— PSALM 121:4

Fear and panic engulfed me as I was walking to pick up my daughter from day care one recent afternoon in Jerusalem. As I strolled down a busy street enjoying the lovely Israeli sunshine, suddenly a loud air-raid siren filled the air. My first impulse was to believe it was just a test, yet reality told me something different.

I froze and anxiously looked around me for some comfort from other people's reactions, yet they were equally petrified. Women were on the ground yelling out prayers, men's eyes stiffly wandered all around searching for a safe place to hide, and children were screaming for fear of what might follow the siren. I was no longer living my comfortable daily life.

After I recovered from my moment of shock, the siren was still blasting. I began to run. I envisioned the face of my beautiful daughter and immediately felt the need to hold her and be with her. I ran past crying children and begged God that my child should not feel this fear. I cried out to God that my child should feel safe — because what in the world could be worse than your child's nightmares coming true without you there to comfort them?

Two minutes into the siren's wail, I arrived at the day care center to find my sweet baby sitting in a circle singing songs with her friends. It was only then that I took my first breath of air after hearing the siren. That is also when the day care supervisor entered the room to tell everyone that the siren that went off was just a malfunction, not a prelude to doomsday.

After experiencing the panic and fear of being helpless in the face of an inevitable incoming rocket, I mourn not only for the innocent Israelis killed but the loss of innocence in the living as well. No longer can mothers take their children to the park, zoo, or restaurant without being conscious of the location of the nearest bomb shelter. No longer can the husband go to work certain that his home and family will be in one piece when he returns.

Haifa residents running for air-raid shelter (ISRANET)

We Israelis yearn for peace so strongly that we're willing to try every possible scenario to reach a lasting peace, no matter how absurd it sounds to some. It pains us deeply to know that if our enemies cherished life as much as they romanticize martyrdom and death, peace would be attainable.

As for now, all I can do is pray and remind myself that it is all in God's hands.

I pray for the people of Israel and long for the day when we will not be awakened by the sound of blaring sirens, but rather the sound of the ram's horn blowing, telling us that redemption has arrived.

GOING DEEPER FOR CHRISTIANS

Think of a time when you have felt your safety was endangered. What did you do? Where did you turn to for help?

Read also:

• Matthew 8:24–26

• John 14:1–3;17: 9–12

FINDING BEAUTY IN EVERY DAY

Although Thanksgiving is not a nationally celebrated holiday in Israel, it is an emotional time for me nonetheless. I use the days to reflect, reminisce, recommit myself to the values that I hold dear, and focus on the many blessings that God has rained down on me. I praise God every second of every day for the beautiful family that He has blessed me with. The lessons I learn regarding God, faith, and worship in my role as a mother and wife are endless, and I thank Him for giving me this enormous blessing.

Yael Eckstein holding young girl at Mevaseret Zion Absorption Center (Debbi Cooper)

The concept of Judaism's focus on praising God and giving thanks was made clear to me a few weeks ago, when I welcomed my four-year-old daughter home from school. She was excited to perform a new song for me that she had learned that day. After picking up her play microphone and putting on her dress-up clothes, she ran

74

to my side and made me focus all my attention on her performance. As she began to sing with animation and intention, I got to my feet to dance. Soon, the two of us were singing at the top of our lungs the words of Psalm 92: "*It is a good thing to give thanks unto the LORD, and to sing praises unto Thy name O Most High*" (v. 1, KJV). With our laughing, singing, and dancing, we were truly making the verses come alive.

This memory is one I will never forget. It was one of those moments where my job as a mother was clear as daylight. God gave me these beautiful children simply to raise them in the vision of God and stamp on their hearts the intention to do His will all the days of their lives. In this moment, God was strongly reminding me that there is no holier job than being a parent.

I am grateful to God for so many things, but this Thanksgiving I have a new resolution. This holiday season my prayers are to find joy and beauty in the typical situations that I too often overlook. This year I will remember that every moment in this world is a chance to rejoice, celebrate, and sanctify His holy name — and I will try my best to make that happen.

GOING DEEPER FOR CHRISTIANS

What makes you want to dance and sing? Together with your family or friends, share the one moment this day that brought you joy. Thank God for that moment.

Read also:

• 2 Corinthians 9:10–12

• Colossians 3:17

• 1 Thessalonians 5:18

• 2 Thessalonians 1:3

THE SECRET TO A LONG LIFE

"START CHILDREN
OFF ON THE WAY
THEY SHOULD GO,
AND EVEN WHEN
THEY ARE OLD
THEY WILL NOT
TURN FROM IT."

— PROVERBS 22:6

What's the key to longevity? Many people would say it's healthy eating and exercise, and, of course, these are important. But spending time with my father's parents, who made *aliyah* (immigrated to Israel) this year at ages 91 and 84, has led me to see that there is a lot more to it than that. They've showed me that unwavering faith

Rabbi Eckstein's parents make aliyah (Yossi Zamir)

and strong family values are secrets to not just living long but living well.

My grandparents' arrival in Israel was remarkable. I'll never forget how, when their plane arrived in Israel, my 91-year-old grandfather danced off and got down on his knees to kiss the holy ground. My grandmother shed tears of joy as she carried her bags off of the plane and walked to passport control. Holding hands, they were greeted at the airport by their dozens of grandchildren and great-grandchildren. "*Your children will return to their own land,*" prophesized Jeremiah (Jeremiah 31:7), and, at the moment of their homecoming, despite their age my grandparents seemed as joyous and excited as awe-struck children.

Since witnessing their miraculous and biblical homecoming just a few months ago, I have visited my grandparents in Jerusalem on a weekly basis. Each visit leaves me more inspired, faithful, and awed. They still study the *Torah* for hours each day, remember the names of each of their 25 great-grandchildren, and call every family member for birthdays, anniversaries, and special events. They live for their faith and their family, and it truly keeps them young. I know this when I see my grandfather's face light up as he tells me about a Bible class he attended, or my grandmother's smile when she speaks about visiting a new great-grandchild. It's then that their secret is clear: If priority is placed on Bible study and family, we will live our lives feeling happy and fulfilled.

Every time I've seen my grandparents they've given me hugs and kisses and told me how much they love me. They've sung prayers to family tunes that have been passed down for generations, and shared Bible teachings to inspire the family. They have held their four children and 13 grandchildren together as one unit through love and respect. As an adult, it is clear to me that much of my faith, my joy for life, my feelings of security and love, can be attributed to the lessons that I have learned from my grandparents.

What a blessing it has been to see how these qualities of godliness and family values have been passed down from my grandparents to my father, Rabbi Eckstein, and then to me and my sisters. My goal is to incorporate these qualities into my daily life. I know that this is an investment that will lead me to a happier and more complete life — and hopefully inspire my own children!

GOING DEEPER FOR CHRISTIANS

Think of the people who have influenced you and encouraged you in your faith. Write notes thanking them!

Read also:

• Ephesians 6:1–4

• Colossians 3:20–21

• 2 Timothy 1:5

INSTILLING A LOVE FOR ISRAEL

> " 'SO THERE IS HOPE FOR YOUR DESCENDANTS,' DECLARES THE LORD. 'YOUR CHILDREN WILL RETURN TO THEIR OWN LAND.' "
>
> — JEREMIAH 31:17

Making *aliyah* to Israel from America was one of the best decisions I've ever made. But it was also one of the hardest. At the young age of 22, I packed my bags, tearfully kissed my family and friends goodbye, and set off to the Holy Land to start life anew.

Thank God, since then my husband and I have been blessed with two beautiful children, who were born in the Holy City of Jerusalem, and have settled into life in the Middle East. We love it here, yet my longing for family back in America is as strong as ever. That is why spending the past two weeks with my sister and her family from America has left me with a joyful heart and peaceful soul.

All year long I eagerly anticipate my family's annual visit, counting down the days until they arrive. Throughout the year, each time I pass a beautiful spot in Israel or take my kids to a fun activity, I remind myself to bring my sister and her children there. I'm deeply aware that seemingly mundane activities like walking in the forest or sitting on the beach become spiritual experiences in the Holy Land. I have become accustomed to encountering these spiritual awakenings at every corner, and I love seeing how visitors' eyes light up as they recognize that, in Israel, we are standing on holy ground.

The first thing my sister always wants to do when she lands in Israel is go out to a restaurant. "The food in Israel just tastes so much better than anywhere else," she always tells me. "Fruits and vegetables especially are amazing delicacies." I get so much joy when I watch her children marveling over cucumbers and tomatoes grown in the Holy Land, and begging me for more after they finish their third serving.

Fresh fruit in Jerusalem's Old City marketplace (IFCJ)

In America my niece and nephew enjoy the modern entertainment of Disney World, movies, and amusement parks, but in Israel they appreciate the return to simplicity. It made me the happiest aunt when they told me that the highlights from their trip were praying at the Western Wall in Jerusalem, running through fields of nettle, and bike riding in the Golan. "I love Israel more than anywhere in the world," my nine-year-old niece told me when we were driving to the airport for their flight back to the U.S. "One day I'll live here!" I looked at my sister's face, and she was smiling proudly as she said, "That was my goal – to instill a love for Israel in my children from a young age."

Although it is hard living far away from family, I realize what an important mission I have here in Israel. By living my dream in the Holy Land, I am inspiring others to open their eyes to the beauty of Israel and to come visit as often as they can. By instilling a love and longing for Israel in the next generation – my niece and nephew – I am clearly seeing the prophet's words come alive: " *'So there is hope for your descendants,' declares the LORD. 'Your children will return to their own land'* " (Jeremiah 31:17).

GOING DEEPER FOR CHRISTIANS

Fill in the blank for your own family: I want to instill a love for _____ in my children.

Read also:

• Colossians 3:16

• 2 Thessalonians 2:15

• 1 Timothy 4:11

• Titus 2:1–8

THE BLESSING OF GODLY LEADERS

> "I WILL RESTORE YOUR LEADERS AS IN DAYS OF OLD, YOUR RULERS AS AT THE BEGINNING. AFTERWARD YOU WILL BE CALLED THE CITY OF RIGHTEOUSNESS, THE FAITHFUL CITY."
>
> — ISAIAH 1:26

I recently was blessed to attend a ceremony at the *Knesset* building in Jerusalem that honored a *Fellowship*–sponsored project called *Tene Briut*, a medical hotline that *The Fellowship* helped set up, so new Ethiopian immigrants can receive lifesaving medical care in Amharic, their own language. *Tene Briut* (words translating to "health" in Amharic and Hebrew) is an innovative project that saves lives every day, and reminds the Ethiopian immigrants from the lost tribe of Dan that they will be cared for here in the Holy Land, and they are not alone.

Ethiopian Jews in Gondar (Ziv Koren)

The emotional ceremony at the *Knesset* opened with a 15-year-old boy singing Psalm 121 in front of five Israeli flags. "*I lift my eyes to the mountains, from where does my help come?*" sang out his sweet voice. "*My help comes from God, who made the heavens and earth,*" he continued singing, and the love for God and the Bible that filled the room of this government building was so evident it gave me chills.

To me, this Israeli boy represented Israel's future, the song represented our unwavering faith, and the *Knesset* building represented our Jewish biblical homeland that has finally come to fruition after 2,000 years of exile.

As I sat in the *Knesset* building and listened to ministers, religious leaders, and new Ethiopian immigrants praise the work of *The Fellowship*'s projects, I lifted my eyes up to the heavens and thanked God for this opportunity to live in the Holy Land, where the highest government officials take time out of their busy schedules to recognize and give thanks to organizations like *The Fellowship* that help strengthen the people and land of Israel. They all commended the work we make possible, and stated that our projects are the culmination of the biblical commandment to "*love your neighbor as yourself*" (Leviticus 19:18).

I was spiritually uplifted when I realized each speech that government officials made had quotes from the Bible, and that they praised God for all of their personal accomplishments. Many ministers wore a traditional Jewish *kippah* (skull cap) on their head to remember that God is always above us and watching over us. Faith and God are not absent from the Israeli government, but are beautifully interwoven within its strong democratic foundation.

It is so awesome and unique to see how the leaders of Israel are enlightened to the fact that ultimately God is in charge and we are only His messengers. Seeing the great leaders of my country put their faith in God and value the work of *The Fellowship* made me feel safe to live in Israel, despite the millions of enemies that surround us.

GOING DEEPER FOR CHRISTIANS

Take time during the week to pray for the leaders of your community, state, and country. Pray that they will rule wisely and righteously.

Read also:

• Luke 20:20–26

• Romans 13:1–7

• Titus 3:1

• 1 Peter 2:13–14

RETURNING TO MY ROOTS

"MAY THE LORD BLESS YOU FROM ZION; MAY YOU SEE THE PROSPERITY OF JERUSALEM ALL THE DAYS OF YOUR LIFE. MAY YOU LIVE TO SEE YOUR CHILDREN'S CHILDREN — PEACE BE ON ISRAEL."

— PSALM 128:5–6

Love for Jerusalem has run through my veins since the day I was born due to my ancestral heritage in the Holy City. Although I was born in America, some of my greatest childhood memories are of taking family trips to the Holy Land and marveling at God's exquisite city. Walking through the narrow, ancient alleyways, I remember my parents telling me that my family heritage goes back 11 generations in Jerusalem.

Old City in Jerusalem (IFCJ)

As a young child, I watched my father talk to old Jerusalemites in hopes of uncovering more information to fill in our family tree. "Of course I know the Eckstein family," the elderly Jerusalem residents would often say as they told us stories about our family that took place prior to the founding of Israel in 1948. Everyone spoke about my ancestors' righteousness, love for God, and commitment to build up the city of Jerusalem as part of a vision of a greater Israel.

During the 11 generations that my family lived in Jerusalem under Ottoman and British rule, they established the first winery in Jerusalem, producing kosher wine for use during *Shabbat* and the holidays. Every time we would drive on the main highway between Jerusalem and Tel Aviv, my father would point to a certain old building on the side of the road and declare with pride, "That is where the first winery in Jerusalem was established by our family, more than four generations ago." He must have told me this dozens of times, yet each time he said it with such joy that I began to feel a new, stronger connection to the Holy City of Jerusalem. This connection allowed me to adapt quickly to life in Jerusalem when I made *aliyah* at the age of 22 – almost immediately I felt at home.

Recently, while in Jerusalem visiting a job training course for newly arrived Ethiopian Jews, I immediately realized there was something special about the building I was in. "This building is one of the oldest in Jerusalem," the director told me, "and it used to be a winery." As the words came out of his mouth, I froze. Suddenly I realized that I was standing in the very spot that my father always pointed to from the car. "This is my family's winery!" I shouted in excitement. After telling him my family story, the director explained to me that two generations ago — before my great-grandfather moved to America — my family sold the building, and it has been changing owners ever since.

Overwhelmed with emotion, I sat down in the middle of the room and closed my eyes in prayer. I envisioned Jerusalem during the days of old — with fewer houses, animals roaming the streets, and merchants selling their handmade goods on every corner. I envisioned my family toiling at the winery making the first kosher wine in Jerusalem. After a few minutes, I opened my eyes and thanked God for bringing me full circle back to my roots, in the Holy City of Jerusalem.

GOING DEEPER FOR CHRISTIANS

Where are your family roots? What about your family heritage — and your spiritual heritage — do you want to pass on?

Read also:

• Romans 8:29

• Galatians 6:9–11

• Ephesians 3:14–19

• Hebrews 2:11

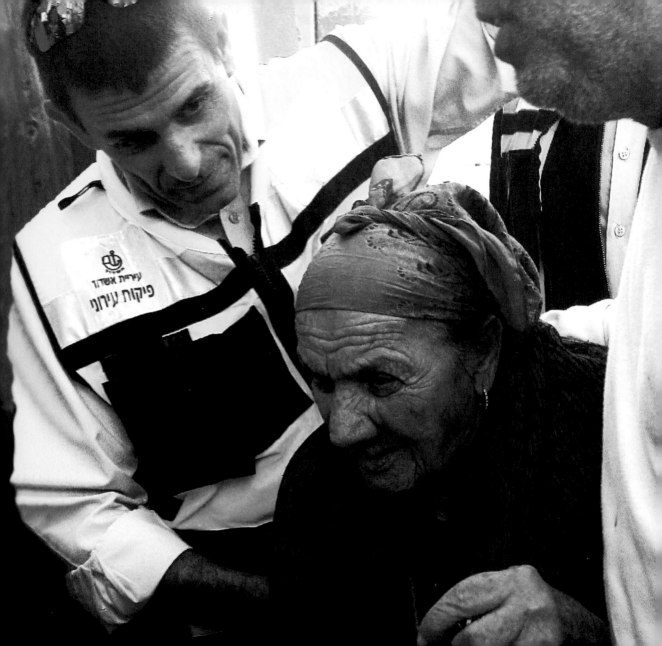

HELPING OTHERS

Even within the beauty and sanctity of life in the Holy Land, unfortunately, there is also abundant suffering. The poverty rates are rising by the year, and the situation for Israel's weakest population – the elderly and children – is growing more unbearable by the day. The *International Fellowship of Christians and Jews* is the leading philanthropic organization in Israel, and provides lifesaving aid to those in need. I am blessed to visit many of the people that IFCJ helps, and I remind them that they are not alone — millions of Christians around the world stand with them and love them, always.

When I deliver IFCJ's emergency aid to needy people in Israel, the stories I hear from Holocaust survivors, new immigrants, and orphaned children often leave me speechless and inspired. In this section on *Helping Others*, come along with me on my visits to those suffering in the Holy Land, and rejoice in the remarkable work we are doing — Christians and Jews together — to fulfill biblical prophecy and obey God's command to love our neighbor as ourselves. ■

85

Spreading Joy

During the Hebrew month of *Adar*, we are commanded by God to live in a state of joy. Unfortunately, at this particular time in my life, the month started as anything but joyful for me.

This surprised me because I'm usually a really happy person. In fact, *Adar* is my favorite month on the Jewish calendar due to its focus on joy. But this year, from the moment we entered *Adar*, I knew nothing but stress.

My husband had come down with the flu at the same time that my children felt ill, and I had a full day of work ahead of me. When I woke up to this reality at 5 a.m., I immediately felt tense. "Please help me, God," I prayed over the sound of my children's cries, and suddenly a little strength came my way. An hour later, I kissed my children goodbye as I left to deliver heating vouchers and food to poor elderly Jews in Israel.

Driving slowly along the narrow, bumpy road, I once again asked God for the strength of joy while visiting several elderly Jews who rely on *The Fellowship* to provide lifesaving sustenance and companionship as well. I was in the middle of this prayer when I looked up to see a brilliant rainbow covering the sky. I felt God's grace as love rained down on me, and I immediately felt the joyfulness of *Adar*!

As a result, I entered the *Fellowship* recipients' homes with a big smile, which brought them joy as well. Throughout the day, I realized a beautiful truth about joy: It's contagious. I felt God's presence everywhere I walked, and the rest of my day was blessed even more. I returned home exhausted, yet with a smile on my face and faith burning in my heart.

As I lay down to sleep that night, verses from Psalm 20 came to my mind and suddenly became real to me in a fresh way. "*May the LORD answer you when you are in distress; may the name of the God of Jacob protect you. May he send you help from the sanctuary and grant you support from Zion. May he remember all your sacrifices and accept your burnt offerings. May he give you the desire of your heart and make all your plans succeed. May we shout for joy over your victory and lift up our banners in the name of our God*" (vv. 1–5a).

That is my prayer for you, that you find delight in answered prayer, strength in the midst of stress, and the desire to spread the contagious nature of God's love and joy.

GOING DEEPER FOR CHRISTIANS

When have you encouraged someone else because of your joy? When has a friend's joy filled you and caused you to rejoice?

Read also:

• John 15:10–12; 17:13

• Romans 12:12

• Galatians 4:22

• Philippians 4:4

TEACHING CHARITY

"GIVE GENEROUSLY
TO THEM [THE POOR]
AND DO SO WITHOUT
A GRUDGING HEART;
THEN BECAUSE OF THIS
THE LORD YOUR GOD
WILL BLESS YOU IN
ALL YOUR WORK AND
IN EVERYTHING YOU
PUT YOUR HAND TO.
THERE WILL ALWAYS
BE POOR PEOPLE IN
THE LAND. THEREFORE
I COMMAND YOU
TO BE OPENHANDED
TOWARD YOUR FELLOW
ISRAELITES WHO ARE
POOR AND NEEDY IN
YOUR LAND."

— DEUTERONOMY 15:10–11

When my daughter turned one, I took her to the market in Jerusalem and gave her some coins. As I watched her hand them out to beggars, I was overwhelmed with pride and joy. In the middle of the bustling market, I took my sweet daughter out of her stroller and danced and sang with her for the *mitzvah* (good deed) she had performed.

There are many values I yearn to pass on to my children, but charity is given strong emphasis in our home. My dream for my children is that they will forever love God and act in holy ways, possessing the positive, God-honoring attributes referred to throughout the Bible.

"Love your neighbor as yourself" (Leviticus 19:18) is a foundational principle of both Christianity and Judaism, and is a teaching my husband and I strive to place deep in our children's hearts. I have clearly seen that the most effective way to present this teaching is by encouraging simple acts of charity.

After my daughter saw the excitement and joy that giving out coins inspired in me that day in the Jerusalem market, giving charity became one of her favorite activities. Now, four years later, when my daughter finds loose coins around the house, she excitedly places them aside for her "giving fund." Giving charity is an act she enjoys and looks forward to, which makes me the proudest mother in the world!

It is no wonder that the Hebrew word for charity — *tzedakah* — literally translates into the word "righteousness." Through this word, the Bible teaches us that if we want to be righteous and holy in the eyes of God, we must be charitable and giving with our possessions.

The Bible also teaches us that all of our possessions truly belong to God anyway. As it is written in Psalm 24:1, "*The earth is the LORD's, and everything in it, the world, and all who live in it.*" I feel strongly that there are few better ways to make God happy than blessing others with the blessings He provides to us. Our loving and giving God wants us to follow His lead of being caring, righteous, and sensitive to the less fortunate.

GOING DEEPER FOR CHRISTIANS

Read Paul's instructions in 2 Corinthians 9:1–15 to the church in Corinth about giving. In what ways does this passage challenge you? In what ways does it encourage you?

Read also:

• Matthew 19:21

• Mark 12:41–43

• Romans 12:8

• 2 Corinthians 8:7

REJOICING IN A NEW LAND

"I WILL SAVE MY PEOPLE FROM THE COUNTRIES OF THE EAST AND THE WEST. I WILL BRING THEM BACK TO LIVE IN JERUSALEM; THEY WILL BE MY PEOPLE, AND I WILL BE FAITHFUL AND RIGHTEOUS TO THEM AS THEIR GOD."

— ZECHARIAH 8:7–8

Jewish tradition holds that when rain falls in Jerusalem, it signals to the world that God is pleased with His children. Rain, the Bible says, is God's way of showering kindness on the people of Israel.

The Holy Land had been experiencing a debilitating drought for years. But I was not at all surprised when I woke up on Tuesday morning — a few

Ethiopian Olim deplaning in Israel (Karen Sandvick)

hours before a historic flight of 81 Ethiopian Jews arrived into Israel thanks to *The Fellowship* — to the sound of thunder and the calming hum of raindrops falling on my windowsill. Not only was I counting the minutes until that miracle flight landed, but God was rejoicing as well!

The prophetic flight was scheduled to land at 3 a.m. and as I pulled up to the airport in the black of night, the words of the prophets echoed in my head: "*I will save my people from the countries of the east and the west. I will bring them back to live in Jerusalem; they will be my people, and I will be faithful and righteous to them as their God*" (Zechariah 8:7–8).

As the first Ethiopian woman departed from the airplane, I had chills —

not from the cold, but from the look on her face as she caught her first glimpse of the Holy Land. She hesitated, trying to absorb the miraculous experience, then fell down on her knees and kissed the ground. Shouting out prayers in a voice cracked with emotion, she praised God, the land of Israel, and the people who had helped bring her home. I stood on the side, waving my Israeli flag in pride and basking in the historic sight unfolding before my very eyes. It felt dreamlike, but what I was watching was real. *"From beyond the rivers of Cush* [Ethiopia] *my worshipers, my scattered people, will bring me offerings,"* Zephaniah said (3:10), and he couldn't have been more accurate.

The most moving moment for me was when an Ethiopian mother saw her daughter for the first time in 11 years and nearly fainted. Her daughter — who was 15 years old when she was left behind in Ethiopia because there was only one spot left on the airplane to Israel — arrived in Israel with her husband and two children. When I asked the mother how she was able to leave her daughter behind and go by herself to Zion, she told me with tears that "the prophets said that we will be reunited in Jerusalem, and I had faith in their words."

As the immigrants walked out through the airport doors to the buses waiting to transport them to their *Fellowship*-sponsored absorption centers, where they would learn Hebrew and receive job training and more, they sang beautiful traditional Ethiopian songs about Jerusalem, freedom, and faith. The words of Isaiah filled my being as I remembered his prophecy of Jerusalem from over 2,000 years ago: *"Joy and gladness will be found in her, thanksgiving and the sound of singing"* (Isaiah 51:3b).

GOING DEEPER FOR CHRISTIANS

Complete the following sentence: "I am most eager for God to fulfill His promise to

_____."

Read also:

• John 3:16; 14:2–4

• Acts 1:11

• 2 Peter 3:13

• Revelation 21:1–4

HELPING ISRAEL'S HOSPITALS

"FOR HE HAS NOT
DESPISED OR
SCORNED THE
SUFFERING OF THE
AFFLICTED ONE;
HE HAS NOT
HIDDEN HIS FACE
FROM HIM BUT HAS
LISTENED TO HIS
CRY FOR HELP."

— PSALM 22:24

When I heard that most hospitals in Israel are not equipped with an MRI machine, I was shocked. MRI machines are one of the most powerful tools for diagnosing various ailments. Israel has one of the best health-care systems in the world, and Israelis have created numerous lifesaving medical devices used internationally. How is it that so many hospitals in the Holy Land are functioning without this critically important machine?

During a visit to Ziv Hospital, located in northern Israel just five miles from the Lebanon border, I discovered the answer to this perplexing question. When I arrived, the waiting room was packed. "You should have seen this hospital during the Second Lebanon War," said Dr. Calin Shapira, the deputy director of the hospital, referring to the dark time when thousands of rockets fired by Hezbollah terrorists fell on the region. "This is the only hospital in the northern region of Israel, so we had all of the soldiers with critical injuries, as well as local residents, coming to us to be treated."

Rubbing his tired eyes, Dr. Shapira told me about the terror that took place during the war, which has left the hospital scared and vulnerable. The terrorists, he said, knew that Ziv Hospital is constantly packed with patients, so they targeted it in hopes of causing as many casualties as possible. He explained that during the war more than 50 rockets landed in the area surrounding the hospital, and the hospital even sustained a direct hit.

A video taken during the 31 days of the Second Lebanon War gave a glimpse of the horror that doctors, staff, and patients experienced. The first two minutes of the video showed patients walking the hallways and doctors helping the sick and injured into hospital beds. Then suddenly terror struck. A loud boom sounded, and then the screen showed the hospital hall fill with smoke. A terrorist rocket had just directly hit the hospital. The security camera showed terrified patients running for safety. The screams of the wounded on that video are still running through my head.

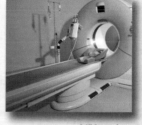

MRI machine

"It was a miracle from God that only a few people were injured," Dr. Shapira said. "It could have been much worse, and we are terrified about what could take place during future wars."

When I asked Dr. Shapira to name the biggest difficulty in treating patients during the war, he explained to me that they were forced to treat Israeli soldiers and citizens without an MRI machine, which often provides the quickest and most accurate diagnosis. He explained that the Israeli government spends so much money on defense and military preparedness that it is unable to provide an MRI machine even to hospitals on the front lines. "MRI machines save lives on a daily basis and especially during war time," Dr. Shapira said.

Just a few days after my visit, *The Fellowship* donated an MRI machine to Ziv Hospital as well as other hospitals on Israel's borders. I am so grateful for the Christians and Jews in America and Canada who give to *The Fellowship*. Their gifts save lives here in the Holy Land every day, and make a tangible difference in alleviating the suffering of the Jewish people.

GOING DEEPER FOR CHRISTIANS

What tangible ways can you help someone who is suffering in your neighborhood? Town? Community?

Read also:

• Matthew 25:36

• Hebrews 13:3

• James 2:15–16

A PROPHETIC HOMECOMING

"HE WILL RAISE
A BANNER FOR
THE NATIONS
AND GATHER THE
EXILES OF ISRAEL;
HE WILL ASSEMBLE
THE SCATTERED
PEOPLE OF JUDAH
FROM THE FOUR
QUARTERS OF
THE EARTH."

— ISAIAH 11:12

Going to pray at the Western Wall in Jerusalem is always an uplifting experience for me, but on this particular visit, I was deeply moved. The Ethiopian rabbis, known as the *Kessim*, invited me to be part of their prayer service at the Western Wall as they celebrated Jerusalem Day.

Dressed in white robes to represent purity, the *Kessim* carefully maneuvered the small cobblestone streets of Jerusalem clutching the ancient prayer books they had used while in exile in Ethiopia. Upon entering the final corridor that revealed a brilliant view of the Western Wall, they broke out

Ethiopian Jews celebrate Sigd (ISRANET)

in smiles and sang songs of praise to God for bringing them home to Israel after more than 2,000 years of exile. I stood on the side crying from joy and thanking God for enabling me to witness biblical prophecy being fulfilled before my eyes.

94

As the *Kessim* approached the Western Wall, they walked slowly, in deep meditation. Visiting this holy site represents the culmination of a dream for these Jews from the once-lost tribe of Dan, and the fulfillment of a prophecy in which they never lost hope.

Throughout their exile, these Jews lived in small villages in northern Ethiopia, where their entire life was dedicated to purifying themselves so that God would grant them the blessing of being reunited with their people and land in Israel. In the synagogue, they would faithfully pray and study the Bible. The stories that were told in their villages were all biblical tales passed down through the generations. Their faith in the God of Israel never died, and their purity persevered.

These Ethiopians experienced the change from primitive villages to modern society overnight when they were miraculously flown to Israel through *The Fellowship*'s *On Wings of Eagles* program. With the help of *The Fellowship*'s support of "absorption centers," designed to help newcomers adjust to life in Israel, I am confident that they will succeed here in the Holy Land and become Israel's future politicians, doctors, businessmen, teachers, lawyers, and more.

As I watched the *Kessim* intently pray at the Western Wall, my own prayers of thanks went up to heaven for *The Fellowship*'s Christian and Jewish donors around the world who made the *Kessim*'s *aliyah* (immigration to Israel) possible. Together we are partners and witnesses to the fulfillment of God's promise to bring His people home.

GOING DEEPER FOR CHRISTIANS

Think of a time when you had a significant homecoming. How did it feel to return after being away? What does it mean to you that we are witnesses and partners in fulfilling God's prophecy?

Read also:

• Matthew 24:14

• Mark 13:10

• Romans 14:11

• Philippians 2:9–11

PROVIDING A HOPE AND A FUTURE

When I visited the *Beit Shanti* home last week — one of the more than 400 *Fellowship*-sponsored projects in Israel — I was blown away. What began in 1992 with one woman's passion for providing homeless youth with a loving home is now a large-scale project that has helped over 24,000 Israeli youth escape homelessness, poverty, and despair.

The youth at *Beit Shanti* share one thing in common: They all have come from difficult and bad circumstances. Many were so badly abused by their parents that they feared death if they remained at home. Others were being raised by drug addicts who starved and neglected them. After these young people fled their homes, many ended up sleeping on park benches and begging for food before *Beit Shanti* stepped in to help.

When I asked how *Beit Shanti* heals these scarred and traumatized youth, the director took me to a long wood table in a beautiful room full of colorful walls and handmade artwork and sat me down. Here, he explained, distraught youth come to know that God loves them, and that there is hope for the future. "God gave us a day of rest each week, so we can start anew for the coming week. At this holy Sabbath table where we congregate once a week to sing, learn, and laugh, our once abused and hopeless youth gain a sense of confidence, faith, and purpose."

As I was leaving, a young man with intense brown eyes stopped to talk to me. "My name is Shaul, and I am the social worker here," he said. "After my father beat me so bad that he broke three of my ribs, at the age of 14 I ran away and lived on the street for five months. *Beit Shanti* was the only place that took me in and provided me with a future."

After meeting people like Shaul and the other wonderful staff, and hearing about the spiritual and academic process that each young person goes through at *Beit Shanti*, I was not surprised to hear that they have an amazing success rate; more than 78 percent of the young people go on to serve in the army, attend university, and live without needing social welfare services. With our support of *Beit Shanti*, it is clear to me that *The Fellowship* and its supporters are planting good seed in good ground, and providing disadvantaged young people with a hope and a future.

Rosh Hashanah *dinner at* Beit Shanti (IFCJ)

GOING DEEPER FOR CHRISTIANS

What do you hope for? Read the Scripture passages below. Based on what you have read, describe the hope you have in God.

Read also:

• Matthew 12:20–22

• Romans 15:13

• Hebrews 6:19–20; 10:23

WARMING HEARTS AND HOMES

It's not every day that I get a hearty hug from an 86-year-old man. But it was an exchange that warmed my heart and made me so proud of the work we do through *The Fellowship*.

Feibel struggles with asthma and relies on an oxygen machine to breathe. When I saw his medical condition and the dilapidated apartment building he calls home, my heart broke. Feibel's small, one-room apartment was freezing cold, and the cracked windows only intensified the chill.

There was a heater next to Feibel's bed, but it was turned off. "I can't afford the electric bill," he explained between big, raspy breaths, "and I have nowhere to turn for help." He showed me the many medicines he must take to stay alive and explained that his only income is a monthly $400 social security check. "I have to decide between buying medicine and food or turning on the heat," he said with tears in his eyes. "So I live in the cold." When I presented Feibel with *The Fellowship*'s $110 (400 shekel) voucher for winter heating, he gave me a huge hug. I could hear his chest whistle with each breath as he joyfully proclaimed, "Maybe now I'll be able to survive these cold months." I answered him with a strong, "Amen!"

Many other residents of Jerusalem were appreciative of these gifts as well. In a show of gratitude for the volunteers walking all over the city to deliver the vouchers, people in their cars honked and waved, passersby offered words of encouragement, and news media swarmed for interviews. The mayor of

Jerusalem even publicly thanked *The Fellowship* for strengthening the nation of Israel through our hundreds of projects, including our program *Winter Heating for the Elderly*.

An ancient Jewish teaching says, "If you have saved one life, it is as if you have saved the entire world." Through projects such as these heating vouchers for the elderly, food boxes for Holocaust survivors, and so many more efforts throughout Israel and the former Soviet Union, *The Fellowship* is saving thousands of Jewish lives every day — and touching the world with these displays of generosity, unity, and love.

Yael Eckstein brings food box to Holocaust survivor (IFCJ)

GOING DEEPER FOR CHRISTIANS

Think of an elderly neighbor or relative you know. How can you help him or her, either with a visit or another act of kindness?

Read also:

• Romans 13:7

• 1 Timothy 5:1

• 1 Peter 2:17; 5:5

A SECOND HOMECOMING

In the aftermath of the deadliest fire ever to hit the Holy Land, the 500 children who live at the *Yemin Orde* orphanage had been evacuated when the blaze threatened their campus, destroying some of the buildings. The *Torah* scrolls also were rescued from the fires. Now it was time to return home.

As I watched the children arrive, it occurred to me that they have survived two devastating losses in their short lives. After being orphaned, they were embraced by the *Fellowship*-funded *Yemin Orde*, only to see it severely burned. Thankfully, *The Fellowship* and its supporters have remained by their side, providing hope and faith during these most difficult times.

Their homecoming was emotional; many of the children broke down in tears upon seeing their homes and earthly possessions turned into heaps of ashes. Surrounded by charred forests that used to be green and empty spaces that were once in bloom with flowers, the children mourned. It was a heartbreaking scene.

Students and Torah *scrolls return to* Yemin Orde (IFCJ)

But amid the darkness was a ray of light. Workers were busily rebuilding their homes, and the staff of the orphanage spoke words of comfort and encouragement. "This is our time of rebirth," the principal of the school gently reassured the children. With great pride, the children stood up and waved their Israeli flags. "*Am Yisrael Chai*" ("the nation of Israel will persevere"), they chanted. It gave me such happiness to see how the orphans had faith in those words.

The orphanage synagogue's *Torah* scrolls came home with the children. Chaim Perry, director of *Yemin Orde*, told me, "The *Torah* scrolls were put in the synagogue before the children went to see their old homes in order to lay a foundation of holiness and faith. If our faith is complete, we can handle anything." The children danced from the entrance of the village down the hill to where the synagogue is located while carrying the *Torah* scrolls.

The party that took place upon reaching the synagogue, which was miraculously spared from the fire, was tremendous. Israeli flags waved tall and proud, children hugged each other, and staff joined the dancing with huge smiles on their faces. It was a celebration of thanksgiving to God.

As I looked at the *Torah* scrolls, I thanked God for instilling such obedience to His words within our hearts. At the same time that the children's evacuation during the raging fire was taking place, plans were being made to save the *Torah* scrolls as well. This action clearly showed the children that we deeply cherish God's holy book. This was a profound lesson for the children during their time of turmoil, one that will stay with them forever: We must turn to God both in times of hardship and in times of joy, just as it says in Psalm 118:5: "*I called upon the LORD in distress: the LORD answered me*" (KJV).

GOING DEEPER FOR CHRISTIANS

When you have cried out to God in distress, how has He answered you? What lesson did you learn from that experience?

Read also:

- Luke 18:1–8

- Romans 8:26

- Ephesians 6:18

- 1 Thessalonians 5:17

CARING FOR OUR HEROES' SONS AND DAUGHTERS

Recently, I had the honor of taking part in a bar and bat mitzvah ceremony for 70 children whose fathers died while serving in the Israeli army. These true heroes of Israel paid the ultimate price defending their country. As I watched the widowed mothers hold tightly to their children's hands with tears streaming down their faces, whispering

IDF soldier in prayer (ISRANET)

to their sons and daughters, "Your father would have been proud," I realized that these children had sacrificed much as well.

In a banquet hall overlooking the Old City of Jerusalem, an army band played Hebrew songs as the children received their bar and bat mitzvah gifts: their own *Torah* and set of *teffilin* (small leather boxes containing parchment inscribed with biblical passages). Tears welled as I saw them wearing their fathers' dog tags. The moment that each father lost his life *l'shem shamayim* — "for a holy purpose" — the people of Israel gained a hero.

During this highly emotional evening, one moment stood out for me. A young man, 13-year-old Gal, stood at the podium during his bar mitzvah and softly said, "Up until two years ago, I considered a bar mitzvah to be a father-and-son event." Despite the deep pain Gal has felt since his father was killed two years ago while on reserve duty, this extraordinary young man still recognizes his father's sacrifice for what it was, and reveres him as a hero. "I want you to know, Dad," he continued, "that I am as proud as I can be when people ask me, 'What does your Dad do?' I answer that you were killed so that we could live — that you were killed for this country."

The reality that the Israeli people face is sobering, yet our faith is so inspiring. Every mother sends her children to the Israeli army for three years when they turn 18, and she watches her husband leave to army reserve duty for one month a year. Though the women know their husbands and children do so for a greater cause — the defense of our beloved Jewish state — the pain that is felt when one soldier falls pierces every citizen's heart.

My prayers at this time are for peace — that no more children will need to celebrate their bar or bat mitzvah without their father, and that we can protect our Holy Land through holy means: love, communication, and brotherhood. May we see the day when our enemies lay down their arms and stop their hostilities against us, the day when we will see fulfilled the biblical promise, "*They will neither harm nor destroy on all my holy mountain, for the earth will be filled with the knowledge of the LORD as the waters cover the sea*" (Isaiah 11:9).

GOING DEEPER FOR CHRISTIANS

What do you think it means to lay down your life for your friends? What have you done, or what has someone done for you, that exemplifies this concept?

Read also:

• John 10:11–18; 15:13

• Romans 5:6–8

MISKANO: A MAN OF MIRACLES

"THOSE THE LORD
HAS RESCUED WILL
RETURN. THEY
WILL ENTER ZION
WITH SINGING;
EVERLASTING JOY
WILL CROWN
THEIR HEADS.
GLADNESS AND JOY
WILL OVERTAKE
THEM, AND
SORROW AND
SIGHING WILL
FLEE AWAY."

— ISAIAH 51:11

When I first met Miskano, I immediately felt a strong connection to him. His warm smile, sweet words, and genuine love for God were infectious. Yet his life story was shocking. Kidnapped as a child by the Ethiopian government, separated from his family for over 40 years, Miskano had been recently reunited with them in Jerusalem thanks to *The Fellowship*'s *On Wings of Eagles* ministry.

Miskano is over 60 years old, yet he clearly remembers as a child telling his friends about his Jewish heritage and his desire to move to Israel. "I was so proud of my heritage, yet in Ethiopia it is dangerous to be a Jew," Miskano explained. "One day, government authorities came to my school and arrested me for plotting against the government. I was only 17 years old, and I was terrified. They took me away to jail and beat me nearly to death. It is a miracle I am even alive."

Miskano was taken out to a field where the authorities were planning to execute him. At the last moment, a Christian police officer guarded Miskano with his own body and would not let anyone shoot him. As Miskano was curled under this man's body, he slipped Miskano a piece of paper with his phone number on it. Miskano put it in his pocket and ran away.

After months of wandering, Miskano joined the Ethiopian army and fought on the frontlines. Many of his comrades were killed in action, yet Miskano miraculously survived. After 20 years of serving in the Ethiopian army, Miskano was released and decided to return to the city where he had last seen his family. He walked for four months, only to find the city deserted.

He feared that his family had been murdered or arrested.

Eventually, Miskano married, had children, and established a life for himself. He told his children tales of his parents and siblings, and together they would pray to one day be reunited. "I was 55 years old, yet I never lost faith that God would somehow take me to Israel. Then a true miracle occurred that changed my life forever."

While cleaning out his children's toys, Miskano came across the phone number of the Christian who had saved his life 40 years before. Miskano called, and to his surprise, the Christian man answered. The man informed Miskano that his family had relocated to Israel. He helped Miskano contact the Israeli Embassy, and officials there told Miskano his family had been looking for him. Within one month, Miskano and his family were flown to Israel and reunited with his parents and siblings.

When Miskano's family in Israel heard that he was alive, they were shocked. His 91-year-old mother was in a nursing home and hadn't spoken for four years, yet when she saw Miskano she began talking again. Two weeks later, she died.

"My whole life has been culminating up to this point," Miskano beamed. "To be reunited with my family, give my mother a final kiss, and walk the holy streets of Jerusalem. A Christian saved my life two times, and I am more grateful to God than words can say."

GOING DEEPER FOR CHRISTIANS

Miskano never lost faith in God and that God would bring him home to Jerusalem. What part do you believe faith plays in miracles? What one thing are you still believing and trusting God to do for you?

Read also:

• Mark 6:4–6; 9:23

• Luke 10:13

• Acts 14:9

A Foundation of Love

"WHEN A FOREIGNER
RESIDES AMONG
YOU IN YOUR
LAND, DO NOT
MISTREAT THEM.
THE FOREIGNER
RESIDING AMONG
YOU MUST BE
TREATED AS YOUR
NATIVE-BORN. LOVE
THEM AS YOURSELF,
FOR YOU WERE
FOREIGNERS IN
EGYPT. I AM THE
LORD YOUR GOD."

— LEVITICUS 19:33–34

I love visiting *The Fellowship*'s projects in Israel and seeing how they are clearly strengthening the Jewish people. Israel's growth, security, and comfort stems, in part, from the support of people who believe in the Bible and God's promise to the Jewish people.

Recently, I brought my daughter to an inspiring event for a *Fellowship*-sponsored program called *Acharai*. The program reaches out to immigrant youth who have been in trouble with the law to let them know that they have not been forgotten and that there are people willing to stand with them on their journey and invest in their future.

Acharai trains the youths both mentally and physically for the army service that is mandatory for every 18-year-old Israeli. For many of these Jewish youngsters, it is the first time in their lives when someone believes and invests

IDF troops entering Ayta a-Shab in Lebanon (ISRANET)

106

in them. The smiles on their faces upon learning they are loved can truly light up the world.

At the event my daughter and I attended, more than 2,500 at-risk youth were inaugurated into elite fighting units of the Israel Defense Forces. I wanted to show my daughter how valuable each individual is and to demonstrate to her the ability — and responsibility — we all have to better the world.

All of *The Fellowship*'s more than 400 projects accomplish the godly mission of strengthening Israel and the Jewish people. Yet there is something about *Acharai* that truly speaks to my heart. Watching these teenagers who once faced such bleak futures now eagerly looking forward to serving their country, I couldn't help offering my thanks to God for this redemptive work.

These soldiers will face the challenging task of fighting terrorism and serving in wars. They will come face to face with people whose hatred for the Jewish people runs deep. Yet, thanks to *Acharai* and those who support it, their foundation will always be love. Throughout their journey in life, they will attribute their successes to God's grace and to strangers who believed in them. This is what I brought my daughter to see: the many sacrifices it took to support the youth along their journey to success, and the ultimate sacrifice that the young soldiers are willing to take to defend God's homeland.

GOING DEEPER FOR CHRISTIANS

Who are the "unforgotten" people in your neighborhood, community, and workplace? How can you reach out to them and provide them with a foundation of love?

Read also:

• Ephesians 2:19–20

• Hebrews 13:2

• 3 John 1:5

MODERN-DAY MANNA

When I pulled up to the *Fellowship*-sponsored Haifa soup kitchen last week, I saw a crowd of elderly Jews outside waiting anxiously for it to open. As the manager of the soup kitchen opened the doors, there was pushing and shoving. The elderly men and women —

Yael Eckstein serves food at a soup kitchen (IFCJ)

many of whom are immigrants from Russia — clearly were desperate to receive their only meal of the day.

I had come that day to help kitchen staff serve lunch to these desperate people. I tried to squeeze through the line of people to enter the building, but they would not let me pass. "I haven't eaten anything since yesterday," I heard one frail man yell out. My heart was breaking as I looked in the eyes of an elderly woman, a Holocaust survivor with numbers tattooed on her arm from a Nazi concentration camp. "This hero who survived the Holocaust should not be begging for food," I softly prayed to God. "That is why you are here," was the answer that penetrated my soul.

Serving the hungry people truly felt like holy work, or *avodat kodesh*, as we say in Hebrew. With each scoop of rice and chicken that I placed on their plates, I said a little prayer. As they sat down to eat their only hot meal of the day, I clearly saw their expressions change from scared, vulnerable, and desperate to hopeful, happy, and content.

As people ate and the pots of food were emptied, I spotted one frail man huddled in the corner. I walked up to him and asked him if he had eaten yet. Embarrassed, he shook his head. This man looked as if he was starving and had red eyes that were full of tears. I led him gently to a table and brought him a plate of rice, vegetables, and chicken. He immediately grabbed his fork and began to eat.

Minutes later when I returned to check on this man, his plate was empty and he was licking his bowl. I refilled it for him, and he gave me a smile that I will never forget.

The food in the soup kitchen reminded me of the manna that God so generously gave the Jews while they were traveling in the desert. Just as we read in the *Torah* that the Jews were alone in the desert, yet were protected by the cloud of glory and the manna that God sent daily, so too these Jews rely on others to live. They left their few belongings in Russia to fulfill their dream of moving to the Holy Land, and are now in Israel alone, with nowhere to turn.

Thanks to God's goodness and the generosity of our donors, *The Fellowship* truly is an organization of hope for impoverished Jewish people not just in Israel, but around the world.

GOING DEEPER FOR CHRISTIANS

How has God provided manna — needed nourishment — for you?

Read also:

- Matthew 6:11

- John 6:32–35

- Revelation 2:17

A BLESSING TO ISRAEL'S ORPHANS

Recently I attended a bar and bat mitzvah for 20 orphaned children. Tears were in my eyes as I sat in the front row of the *Fellowship*-sponsored *Neve Michael* orphanage watching the children dance, sing, and praise God for bringing them to this holy day marking their entry into adulthood.

The atmosphere at *Neve Michael* was celebratory. Balloons were tied to the tables, children were dressed in nice clothing, and musicians played Jewish songs of celebration. The children were dancing and laughing. In many ways it felt like a typical bar mitzvah. Yet a closer look revealed the pain that many of the children were carrying inside — at this milestone event in the children's lives, parents were absent.

As I sat with Hava, the director of the orphanage, a beautiful 12-year-old girl named Rivka came over to give her a big hug. As the girl walked off I noticed she was crying. Hava explained to me that eight years ago Rivka and her three siblings witnessed their father murder their mother. Their father died in prison just a few years later.

I was deeply shocked to think of the hardship Rivka has experienced at such a young age. Hava told me that staff at *Neve Michael* has focused on rebuilding Rivka's life. "Today, Rivka is celebrating her bat mitzvah with every single person here as her supportive and loving family," she said. "That is what *Neve Michael* creates for these children — a stable family environment."

"HE DEFENDS THE CAUSE OF THE FATHERLESS AND THE WIDOW, AND LOVES THE FOREIGNER RESIDING AMONG YOU, GIVING THEM FOOD AND CLOTHING."

— DEUTERONOMY 10:18

Sitting to my left was a row of adults, graduates of *Neve Michael* who had come back to serve as role models for the next generation of students. Each one that I spoke to had a good job, a healthy outlook, and a stable family life, and they attributed their success to *Neve Michael*. I was reminded how crucial *Fellowship* funding is to *Neve Michael*, and what an awesome responsibility God has given us to ensure that schools like this continue to operate.

As the children got up to speak at the event, they were glowing with pride.

Children eating in Fellowship-*sponsored orphanage*
(FJCIS)

The orphanage had bought each of them new clothes and a special ring as a present. One by one, they thanked God, *Neve Michael*, and *The Fellowship*'s supporters for helping them during their darkest times by providing the security of a home, food, education, and love — basic things that they don't take for granted.

My visit to *Neve Michael* was bittersweet. I cried to God for the pain and anguish that these young people have experienced. Yet I also thanked Him for enabling *The Fellowship* to relieve some of their worry and play a role in shaping the children of Israel into well-established, emotionally healthy, and productive citizens.

GOING DEEPER FOR CHRISTIANS

Consider how you might encourage the children and young people in your community who are at risk.

Read also:

• John 14:18

• Romans 12:13

• James 1:27

SURVIVING ON FAITH

"HE UPHOLDS THE

CAUSE OF THE

OPPRESSED AND

GIVES FOOD TO

THE HUNGRY."

— PSALM 146:7a

It was my first time visiting Kiryat Shmona — an Israeli town less than two miles from the Lebanon border — and I must admit I was a little nervous. Kiryat Shmona has been a frequent target for terrorist rockets and other cross-border attacks. It is also a poverty-stricken town inhabited by a large population of elderly Russian immigrants. I was there, despite Arab riots taking place in Lebanon on that day, to ensure that these immigrants were being fed and cared for in their final years.

I arrived at the *Fellowship*-sponsored soup kitchen in Kiryat Shmona at 8 a.m., and the atmosphere was hectic. Two cooks were racing with the clock to finish preparing 650 hot meals by lunchtime, and volunteers lined up at the door were packaging the food in takeaway containers. "Many of the people we feed are too sick to leave their houses, so we bring the food to them," explained a young woman with a warm smile, while carrying ten meals to her car. "I can tell you firsthand that the people who receive this food daily would starve without it. What *The Fellowship* is doing here is the most important work in the world: feeding the hungry."

Around 11 a.m. I left the heat of the kitchen to visit one of the recipients of these daily meal deliveries. I walked up five flights of stairs in a rundown, moldy apartment building, then entered the small, one-room apartment of 85-year-old Ziv, a Holocaust survivor who has diabetes and heart disease and is bedridden. That is when the words of the worker at the soup kitchen truly hit home.

When Ziv saw me holding the food, his sad face suddenly broke into a smile. "I haven't eaten since a meal was brought to me yesterday," he said. "I can't leave my apartment or afford help, and without these meals I would be forgotten and starve." With a big hug, I handed him the warm chicken, rice, and vegetables and sat with him to keep him company while he ate.

Before leaving Kiryat Shmona, the director of the soup kitchen pulled out a huge folder that holds food requests and began reading me desperate letters from people begging for help. "We work in this little kitchen day and night to provide 650 daily meals to the residents," he explained, "yet we have 1,200 daily requests for food."

The need here, and throughout Israel, remains great. Since my visit to Kiryat Shmona, I have been praying to God for Ziv and all of the other needy people who struggle to survive each day. With God's help — and the generosity of *Fellowship* supporters — we pray we will be able to reach out to the hungry people in Israel and alleviate their suffering through food packages and love.

Poverty on the streets of Israel (Ziv Koren)

GOING DEEPER FOR CHRISTIANS

Look for opportunities in your community to help those who are hungry. Volunteer your time, or donate some food items to your local food pantry.

Read also:

• Matthew 15:32; 25:35

• James 2:15–16

• 1 John 3:17

THE BLESSING OF A HOME

> "CHILDREN ARE
> A HERITAGE
> FROM THE LORD,
> OFFSPRING
> A REWARD
> FROM HIM."
>
> — PSALM 127:3

Being the mother to my beautiful children is my most precious responsibility. My husband and I recognize how blessed we are that God granted us the sacred task of nurturing His holy creations. We do everything in our power to live up to our responsibility as parents, which is an exhausting — but deeply rewarding — duty. During the round of endless tasks

Young Israeli boy (JDC)

that I perform daily, I say a little prayer that God will grant me the strength to continue fulfilling these responsibilities for as long as my children need me.

The biggest fear for parents is that they will not be able to provide for their child's emotional and physical needs — just as every child's deepest fear is losing a parent's loving care. So, as a mother, I have a special place in my heart for children who have no parents. Each time I visit one of *The Fellowship*'s many facilities for orphans in Israel, I scrutinize every aspect of the operation on behalf of all the children living there who have no one to speak out for them.

During a recent visit to one of these orphanages, I passed through a gate covered with beautiful paintings of children playing. Entering the grounds, I felt warmth and energy. Children who appeared to range in age from five to about 13 played on the grass, throwing balls, singing songs, and laughing together.

As the end-of-recess bell sounded, they ran back inside the school building to attend their classes. The scene was so different from what many people imagine orphanages to be — depressing and somber places without laughter and love.

This joyful atmosphere is the result of a policy implemented to ensure the highest level of care for these precious children of Israel. The children at this orphanage don't sleep in massive dorms or eat in cafeterias, but live in homes. *The Fellowship* has hired an adoptive "mother and father" — a married couple — who live onsite with the children to provide for all of their needs.

This "family" cooks and eats dinner together, helps each other with homework, and shares household chores. The adoptive parents patiently tuck each child into bed every night, and are there to listen to them when they need a friendly ear or a shoulder to cry on. This new model for an orphanage offers an atmosphere of security and love to emotionally broken children, instilling in them the confidence they need in adulthood to establish a career and raise secure families of their own.

It is clearly having an impact. During my visit, I spoke with a 10-year-old boy who had entered the orphanage the week prior, after his father lost a five-year battle with cancer. This child, who immigrated to Israel six years ago from the former Soviet republic of Georgia, explained to me how he used to have nightmares about his father dying. "I envisioned myself living on the streets and starving to death," he told me as tears ran down his face. "This orphanage is the biggest blessing for me because I am provided with everything I need. They make me feel loved and welcome. I wish I was at home with my dad, but the people here treat me like family."

GOING DEEPER FOR CHRISTIANS

Make a list of the many blessings you have experienced from being part of your biological family, your church family, and God's family.

Read also:

- John 1:12
- Romans 8:15–16
- Galatians 4:6–7
- Hebrews 2:11

Bringing Blessings to the Holy Land

Recently my father, Rabbi Eckstein, and I have been busy planning new and innovative aid projects to provide hope to the Holy Land and to remind her residents that they are not alone. Through the more than 400 *Fellowship* projects in Israel, the Jewish people are keenly aware that we have Christian friends around the world who strongly stand with Israel during this difficult time.

Because my father and I live in Israel and see the desperate needs of the elderly, immigrants, and children firsthand, it's easy for us to quickly identify how *The Fellowship* can effectively provide lifesaving aid. Throughout the year, *The Fellowship* provides aid to tens of thousands of Israel's poorest residents. As soon as we identify a desperate need, we meet with other *Fellowship* staff to put together a cost-effective project to alleviate the suffering.

Yael Eckstein helps with blanket distribution
(Debbi Cooper)

After my father and I visited the homes of some elderly Israelis during the cold winter months and saw that they were very cold because they couldn't afford

116

heat or even blankets, *The Fellowship* began a mass distribution of thousands of heavy blankets. While distributing these blankets, I met elderly women who were bedridden from illness. Prior to the project, many of them had been living alone with no blankets at all. Thank God that being here on the ground in Israel enabled us to meet a need that no one would have otherwise known about!

I feel good about our efforts, which are made possible by our ministry partners, and by knowing that *The Fellowship* works closely with local officials to receive information about the neediest residents in particular cities. In this way, we can ensure that each recipient of our aid is indeed needy and is also already receiving the services to which he or she is entitled. Unfortunately, because of the security needs in Israel, the government does not have sufficient funds left to alleviate the many crucial needs of her people, leaving many residents desperate for help.

Wherever I travel around the country, it is clear to me that *The Fellowship* is known by everyone in Israel for providing lifesaving aid to needy people who have nowhere else to turn. When I look in the eyes of *Fellowship* aid recipients and they tell me how Christians in America were there for them during their hardest moments in life, I know that *The Fellowship* is doing the most blessed work in the world.

We are simply the messengers of these blessings. We are so thankful that *The Fellowship*'s partners in America and around the world are responding to God's call to bless His children: "*I will bless those who bless you, and whoever curses you I will curse*" (Genesis 12:3).

GOING DEEPER FOR CHRISTIANS

What blessings have you received when you have helped God's people? Share with someone you know why it's important to support Israel and her people.

Read also:

- Luke 6:38

- Acts 20:35

- Romans 15:27

A JOYFUL REUNION

"THEN THEY WILL KNOW THAT I AM THE LORD THEIR GOD, FOR THOUGH I SENT THEM INTO EXILE AMONG THE NATIONS, I WILL GATHER THEM TO THEIR OWN LAND, NOT LEAVING ANY BEHIND."

— EZEKIEL 39:28

Every immigrant to Israel has a story of *aliyah* (immigration to Israel) to tell. Though happy to finally call Israel home, they often make enormous sacrifices to leave the country where they were born, breaking bonds of family and culture in order to fulfill the words of the prophets. Meeting one of these immigrants, Atrasu, left me praying to God for all of the other Jewish Ethiopians who yearn to return to Jerusalem.

Atrasu is a sweet, soft-spoken Ethiopian man who lives in Jerusalem and works at a Jewish bookstore. He arrived in Israel four years ago with his young child and beautiful wife after a harrowing journey and nearly 12 years of waiting.

Eleven years ago, the people of Atrasu's rural village packed their bags and began walking. They intended to finally fulfill their lifelong desire to go to Israel. Atrasu told me that "throughout our exile we believed we would one day be reunited with the rest of the Jewish people in Jerusalem. But it was illegal to leave our village. We knew that trying to walk to Israel was dangerous, but we'd been waiting 2,000 years for this reunion." To avoid detection, the people broke into small groups for the journey, and Atrasu and his family were separated from his parents.

Atrasu and his wife and child walked for three months to get to the Ethiopian capital, Addis Ababa. During the day they would bury themselves in the sand in order to avoid the authorities, and at night they would walk. "We were traveling with my sister, her husband, and their two children," Atrasu said. "On the way, my sister died. She was pregnant and didn't have the energy to endure the journey."

After arriving in Addis Ababa, Atrasu and his family waited more years for the opportunity to make *aliyah*. "Finally, we came to Israel through *The Fellowship*'s *On Wings of Eagles* program," he said. "But we had to leave my brother-in-law and nieces behind. They are still waiting in Ethiopia in poverty and fear to come home to Israel."

During this time, Atrasu had no word on the fate of his parents. Finally, after arriving in Israel, he found out they had survived the journey from their village and had gotten safely to the Ethiopian city of Gondar. But they, too, would have to wait years before the opportunity came to escape Ethiopia and travel to the Promised Land.

Ethiopian Jews await immigration to Israel (Ziv Koren)

"From the day I arrived in Israel, I prayed for my parents to come home to Israel. Just two weeks ago they arrived," Atrasu said, the emotion evident in his voice. "They waited 11 years for this opportunity."

Atrasu's story is repeated over and over through *On Wings of Eagles*. Thousands of Jews from all over the world have escaped persecution, anti-Semitism, and poverty through this ministry. I know that one day all the Jewish people — including Atrasu's brother-in-law and nieces — will come home because the Bible tells us, *"Then they will know that I am the LORD their God, for though I sent them into exile among the nations, I will gather them to their own land, not leaving any behind"* (Ezekiel 39:28).

GOING DEEPER FOR CHRISTIANS

The ingathering of Jews from the four corners of the world is a poignant reminder that our God is faithful and keeps His promises. What promise are you waiting on from God? How does Atrasu's story encourage you?

Read also:

• Luke 1:45

• Acts 2:38–39

• Romans 15:8

• 2 Corinthians 1:20